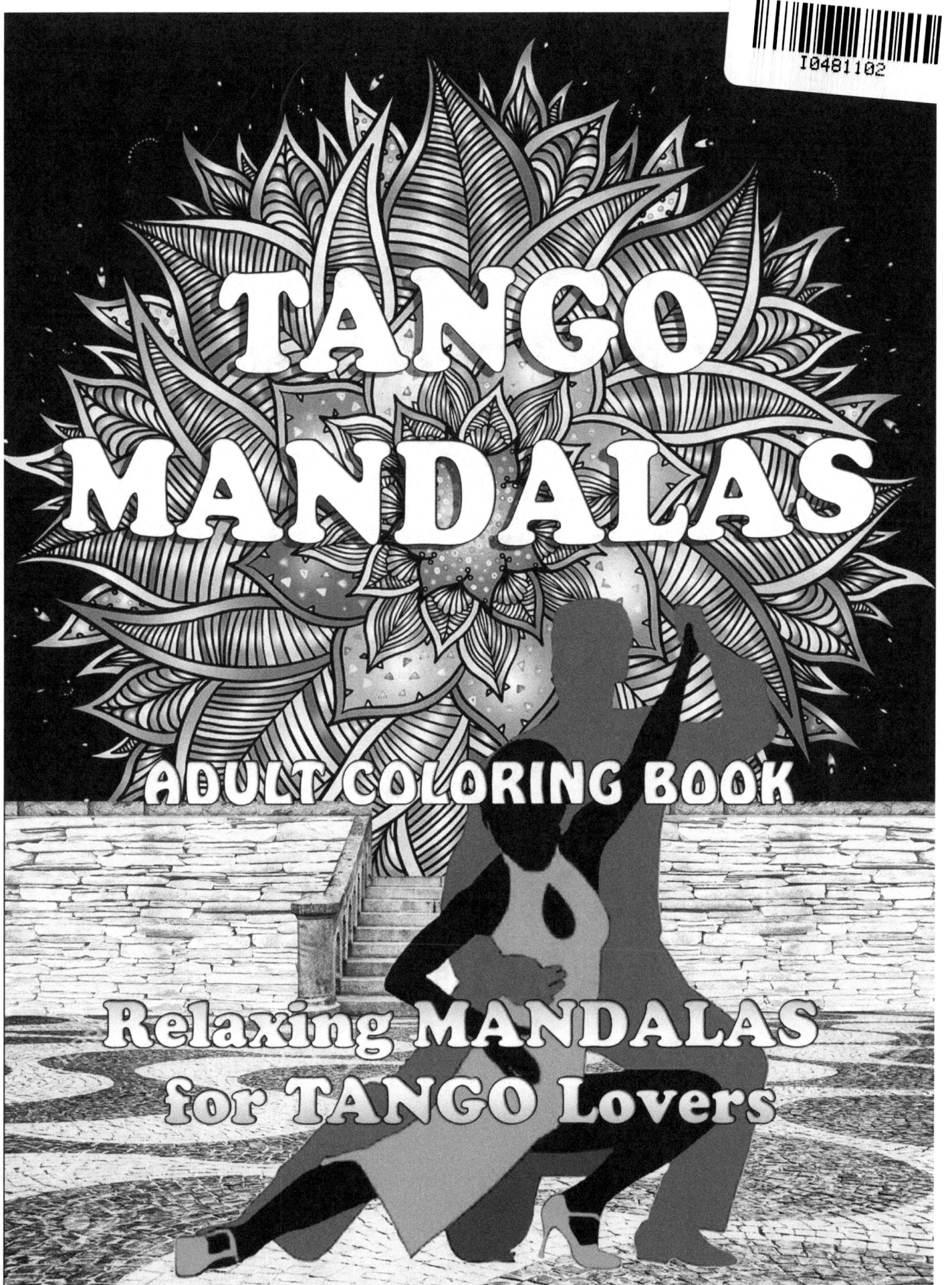

TANGO MANDALAS

ADULT COLORING BOOK

Relaxing MANDALAS for TANGO Lovers

TANGO MANDALAS

ADULT COLORING BOOK

Relaxing MANDALAS for TANGO Lovers

Beautiful Mandalas coloring book, with a unique style of relaxing drawings from the publishing brand *Ryan Avas*. 40 original mandalas with tango figures that will encourage your creativity.

Relax and enjoy while coloring our book **"TANGO MANDALAS. Adult Coloring Book. Relaxing MANDALAS for TANGO Lovers"**, with a variety of fantastic anti-stress mandalas that will color your inspiration.

Take your drawing supplies and create your own art collection. The **TANGO MANDALAS** book promises hours of fun and relaxation for colorists of all ages.

Let your imagination run wild and…

Enjoy it!

Ryan Avas

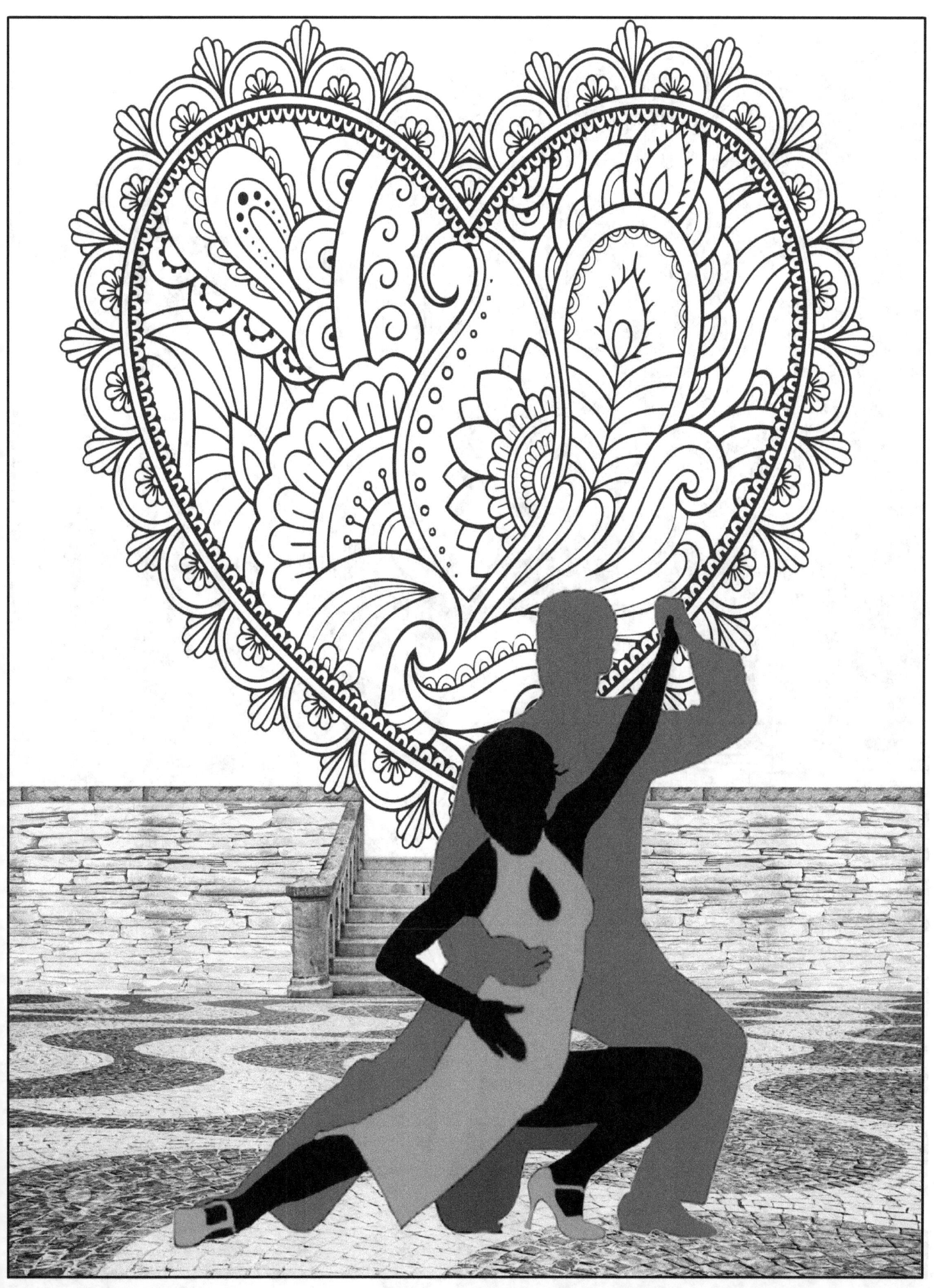

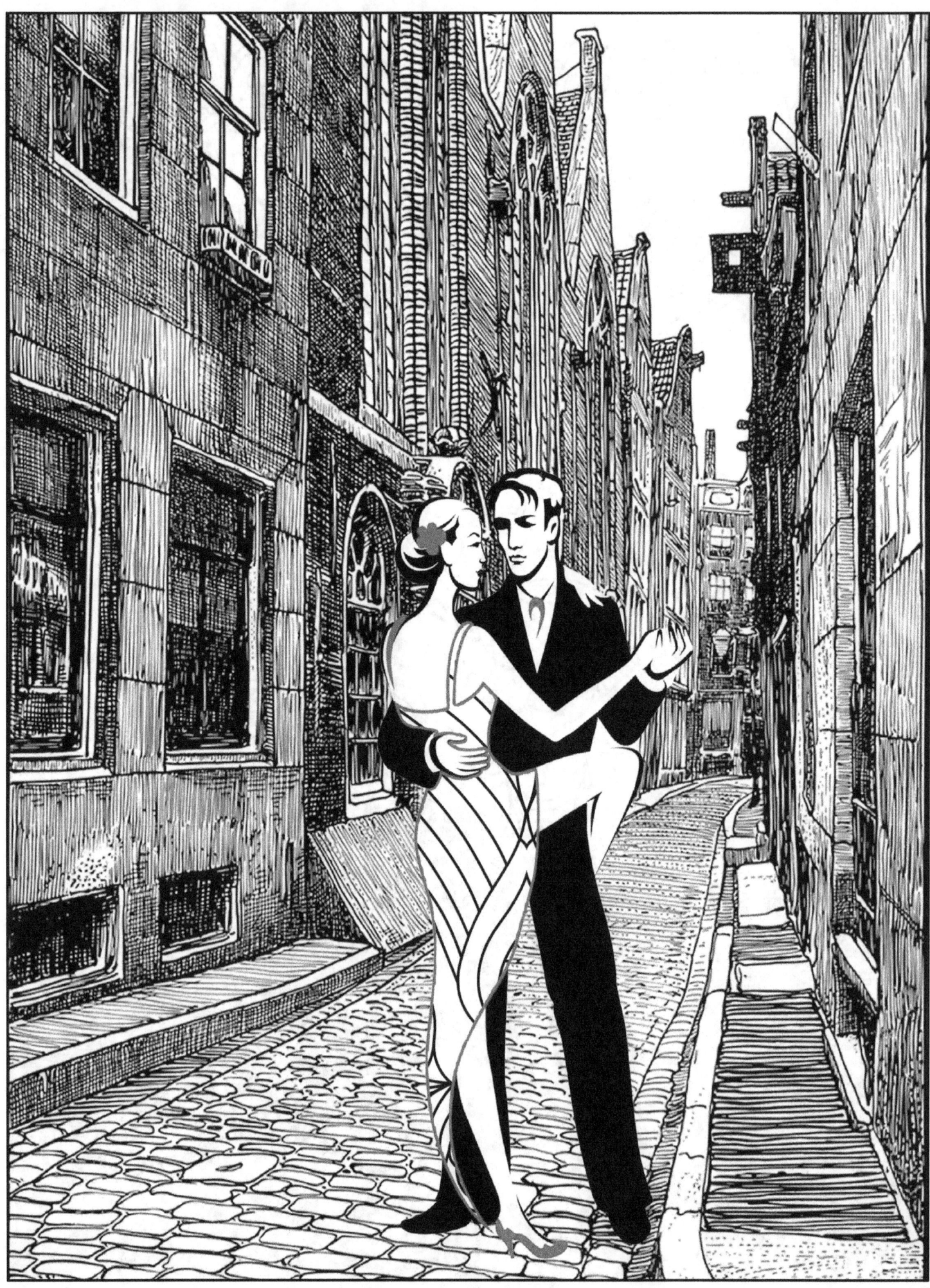

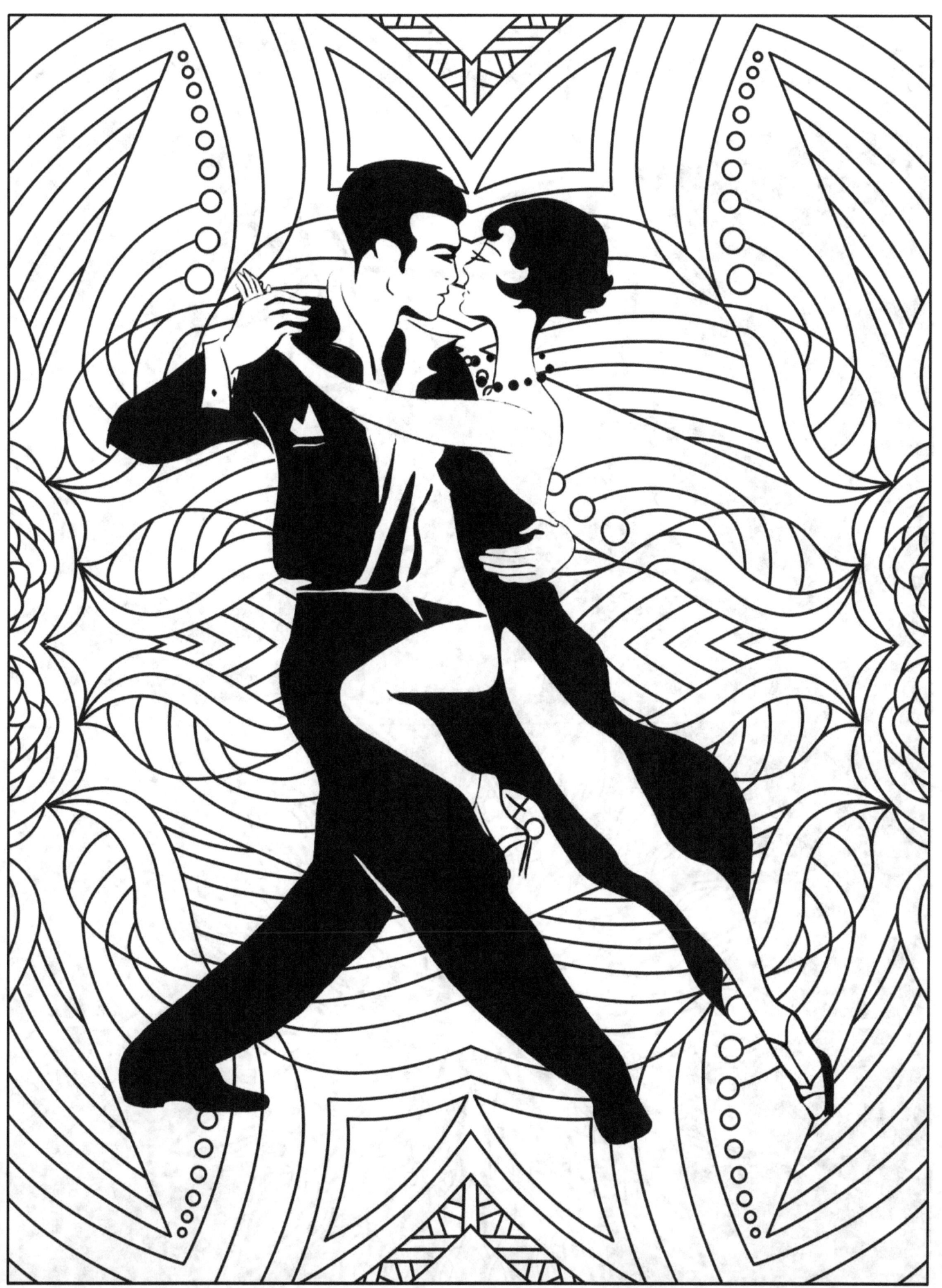

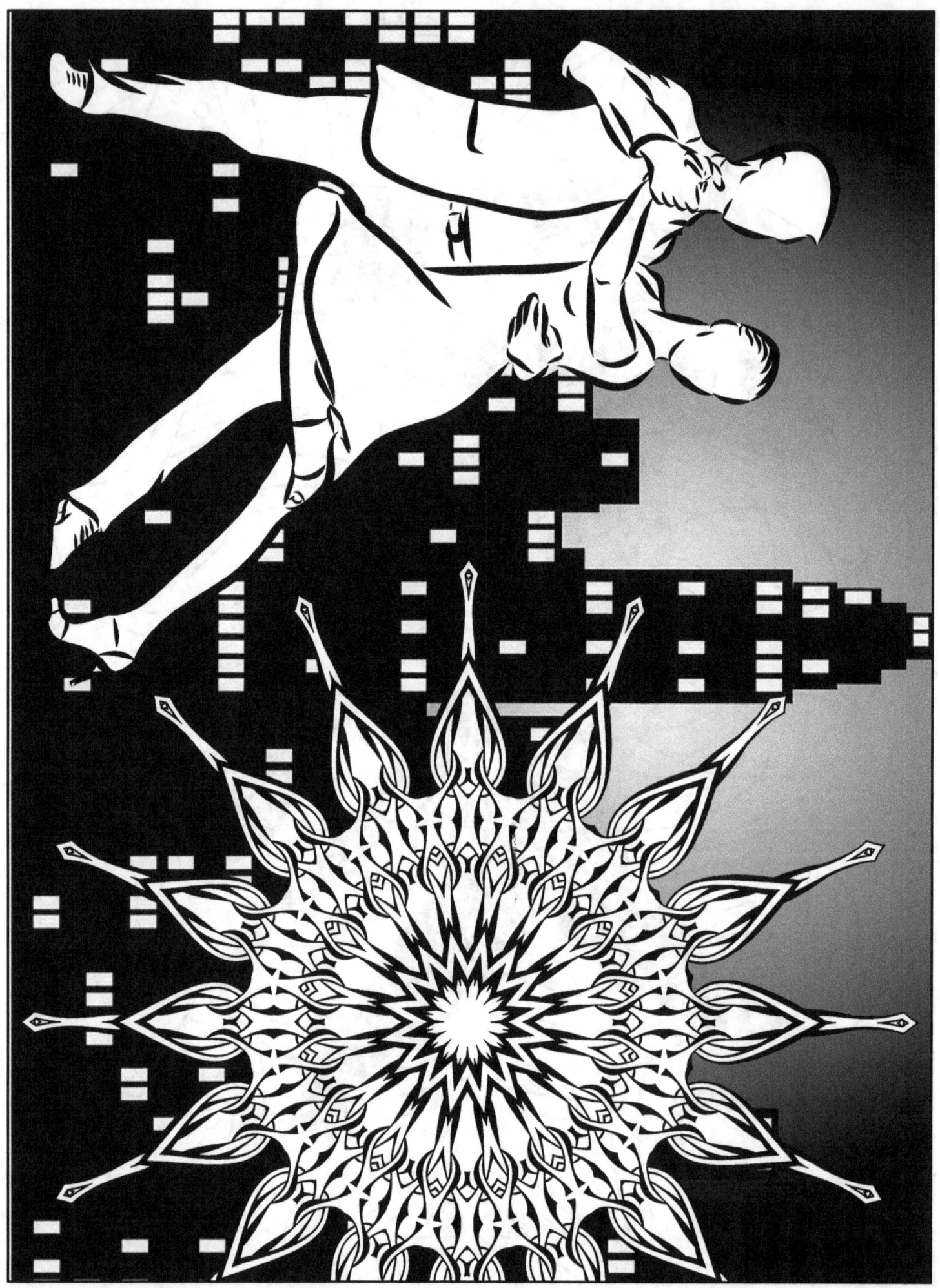

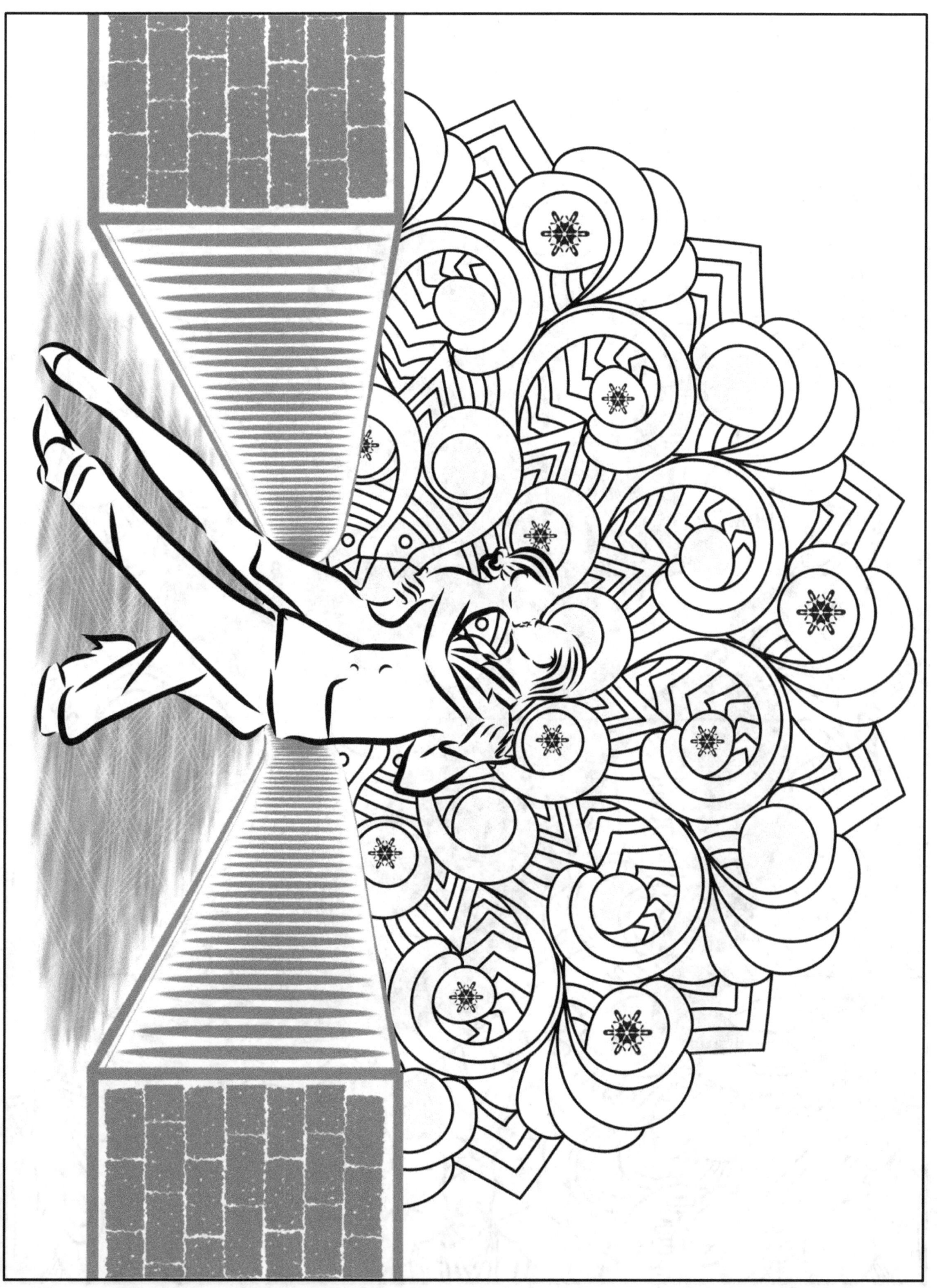

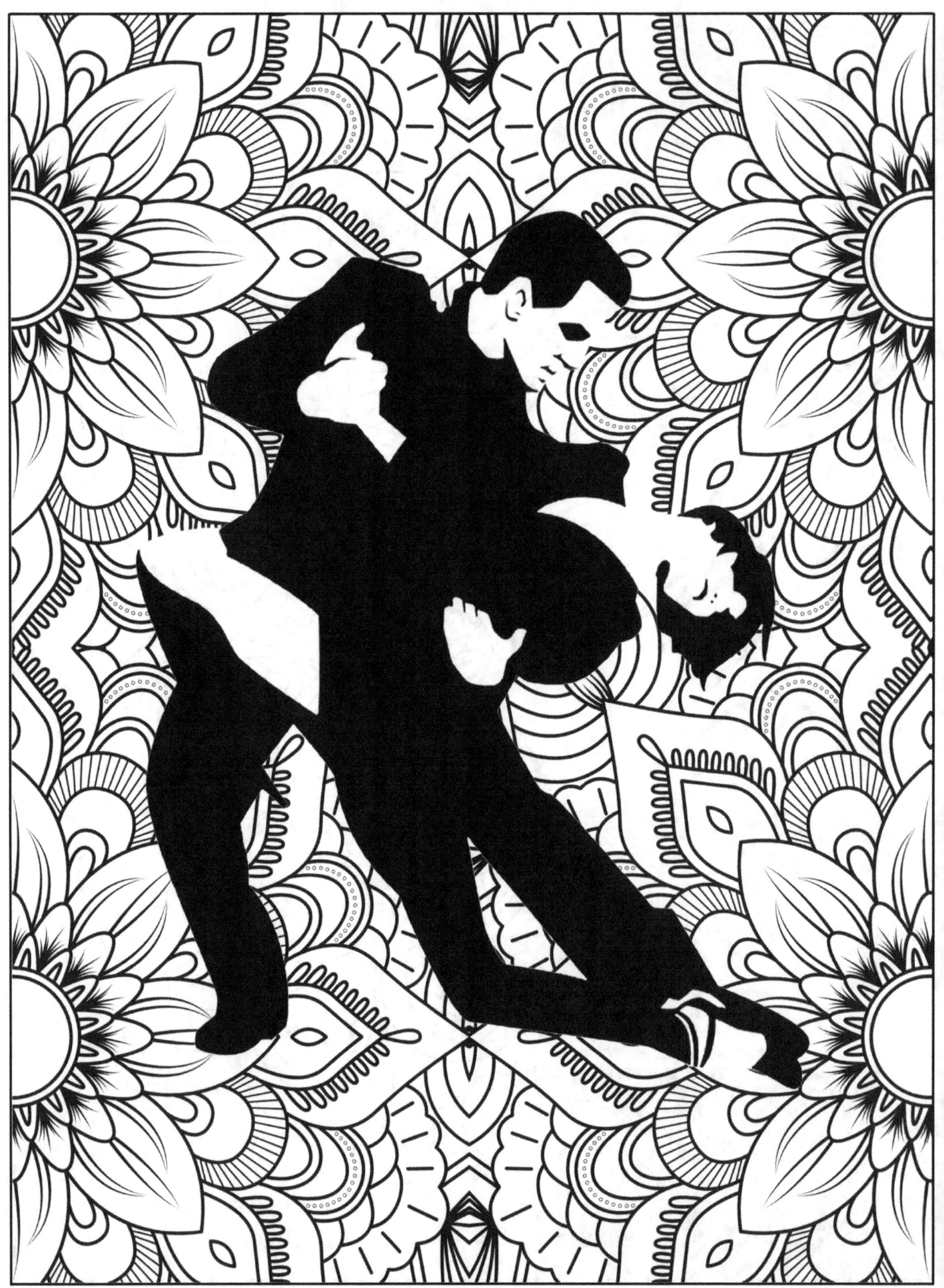

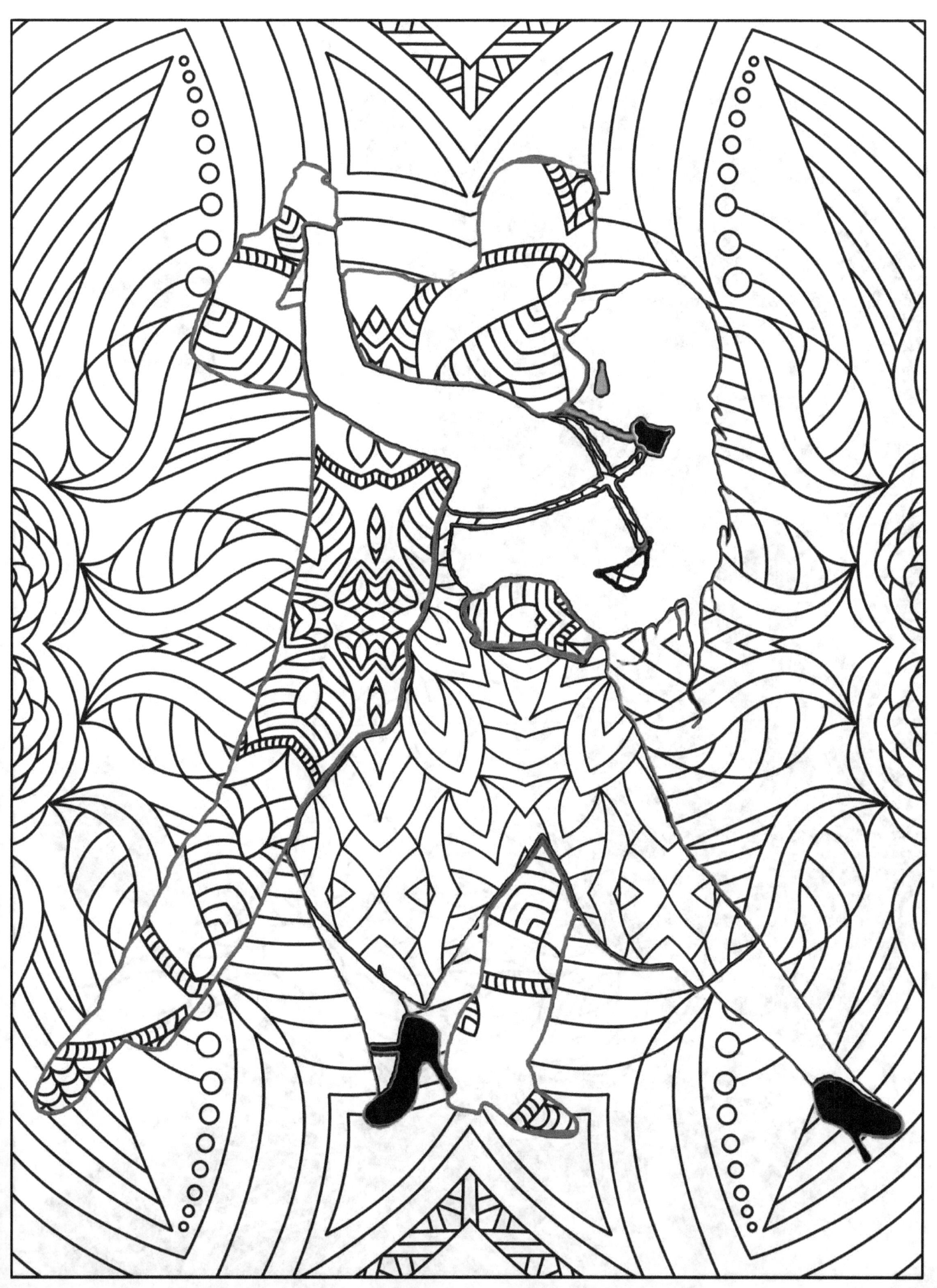

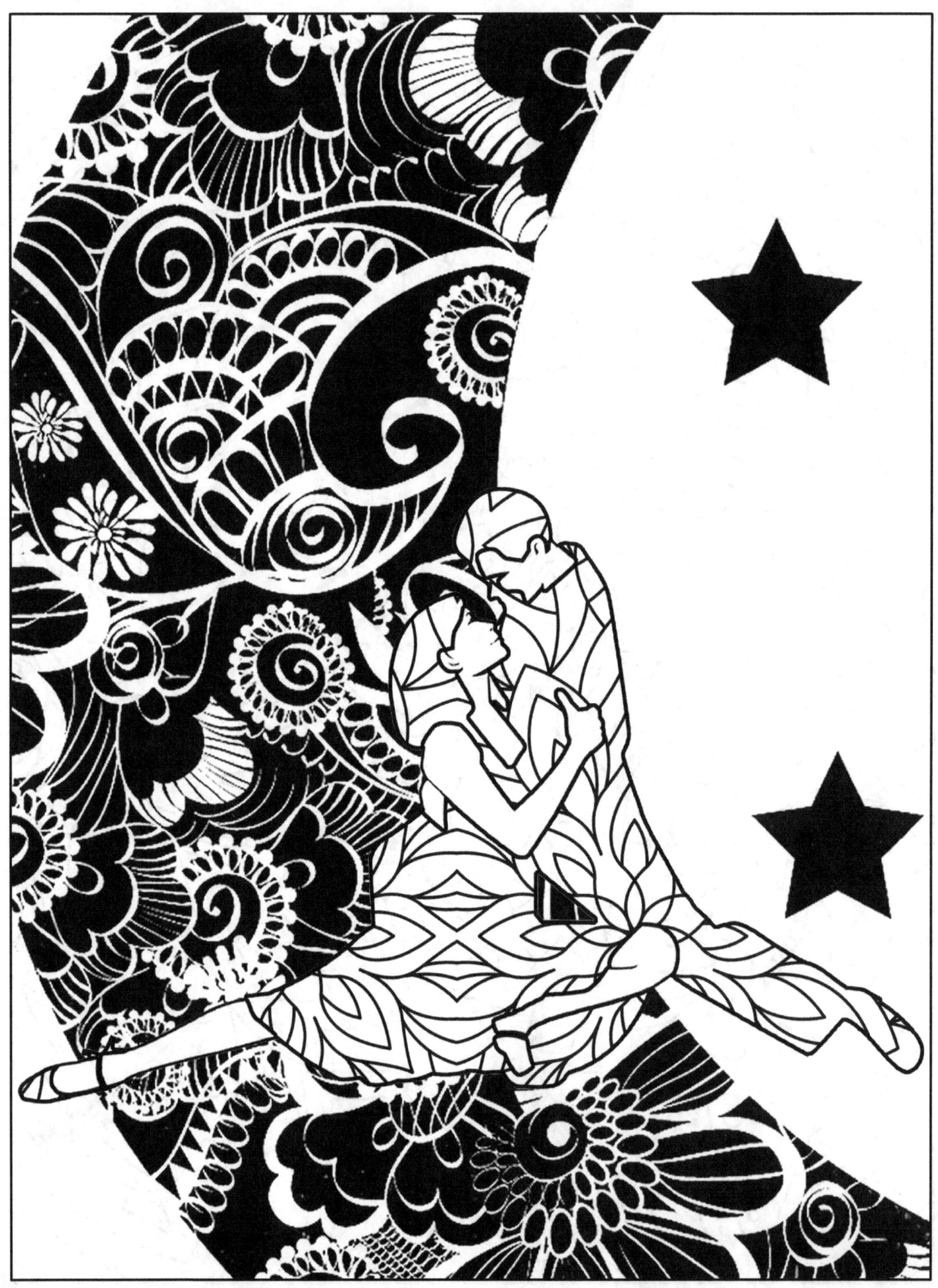

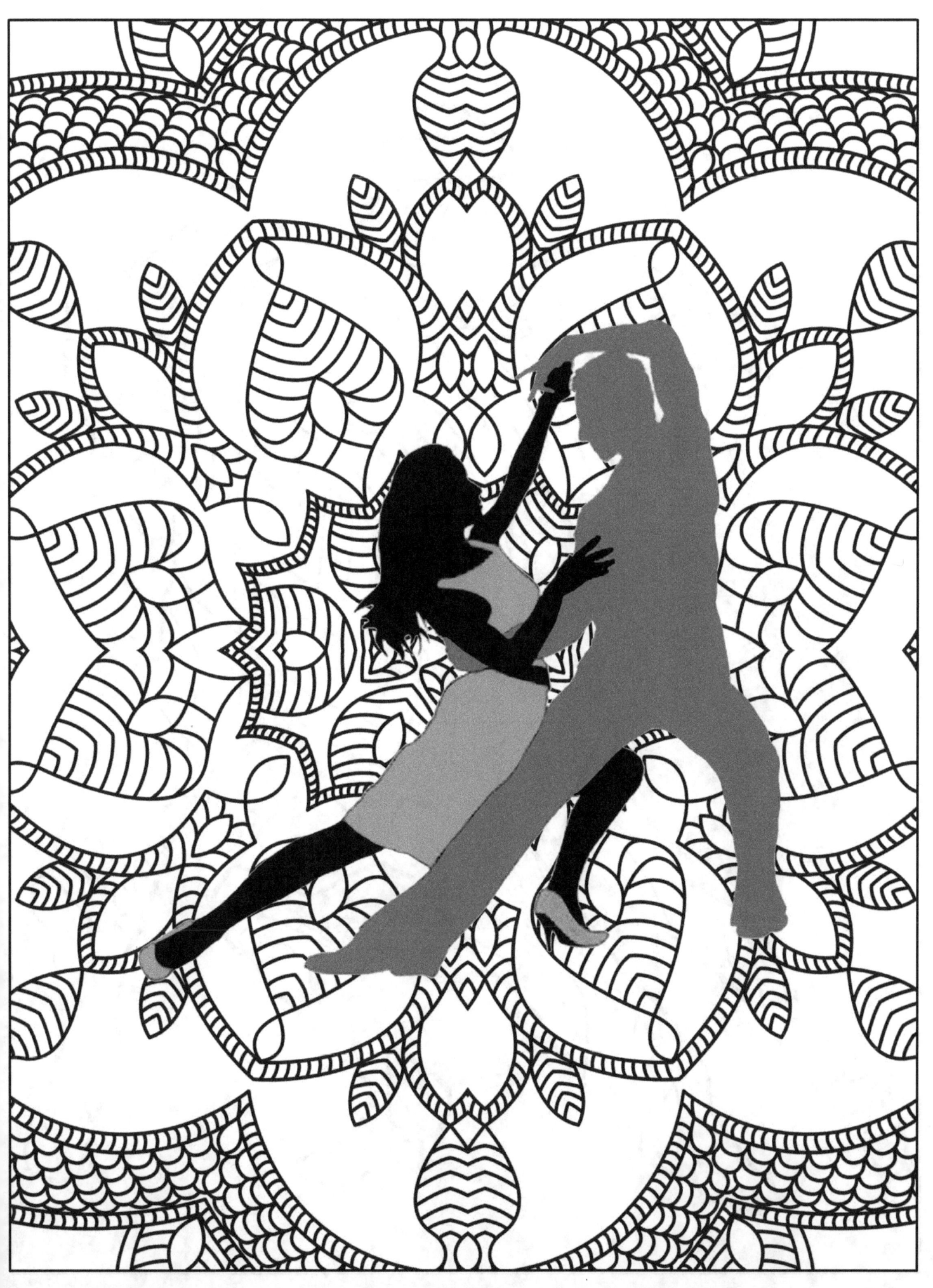

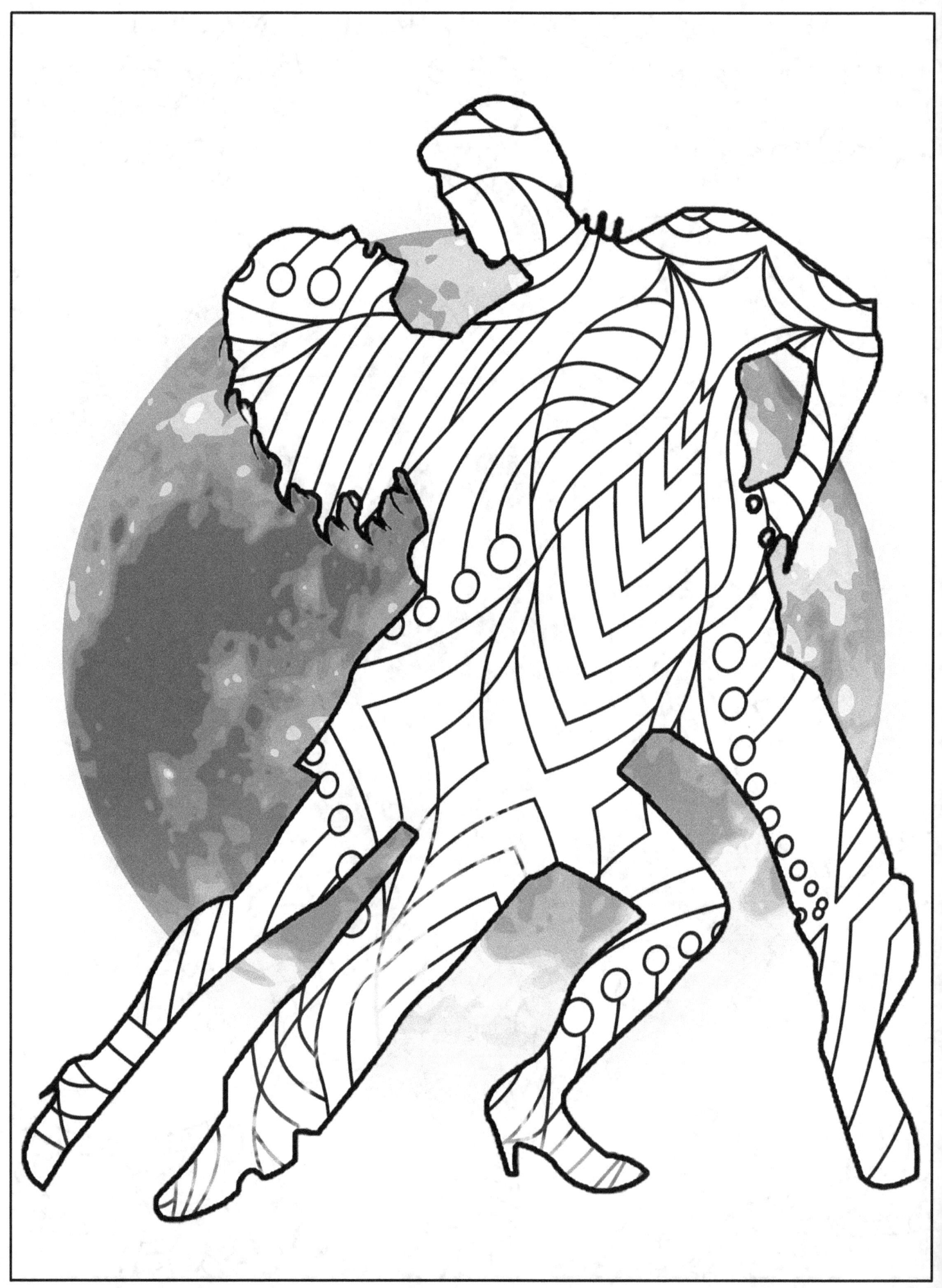

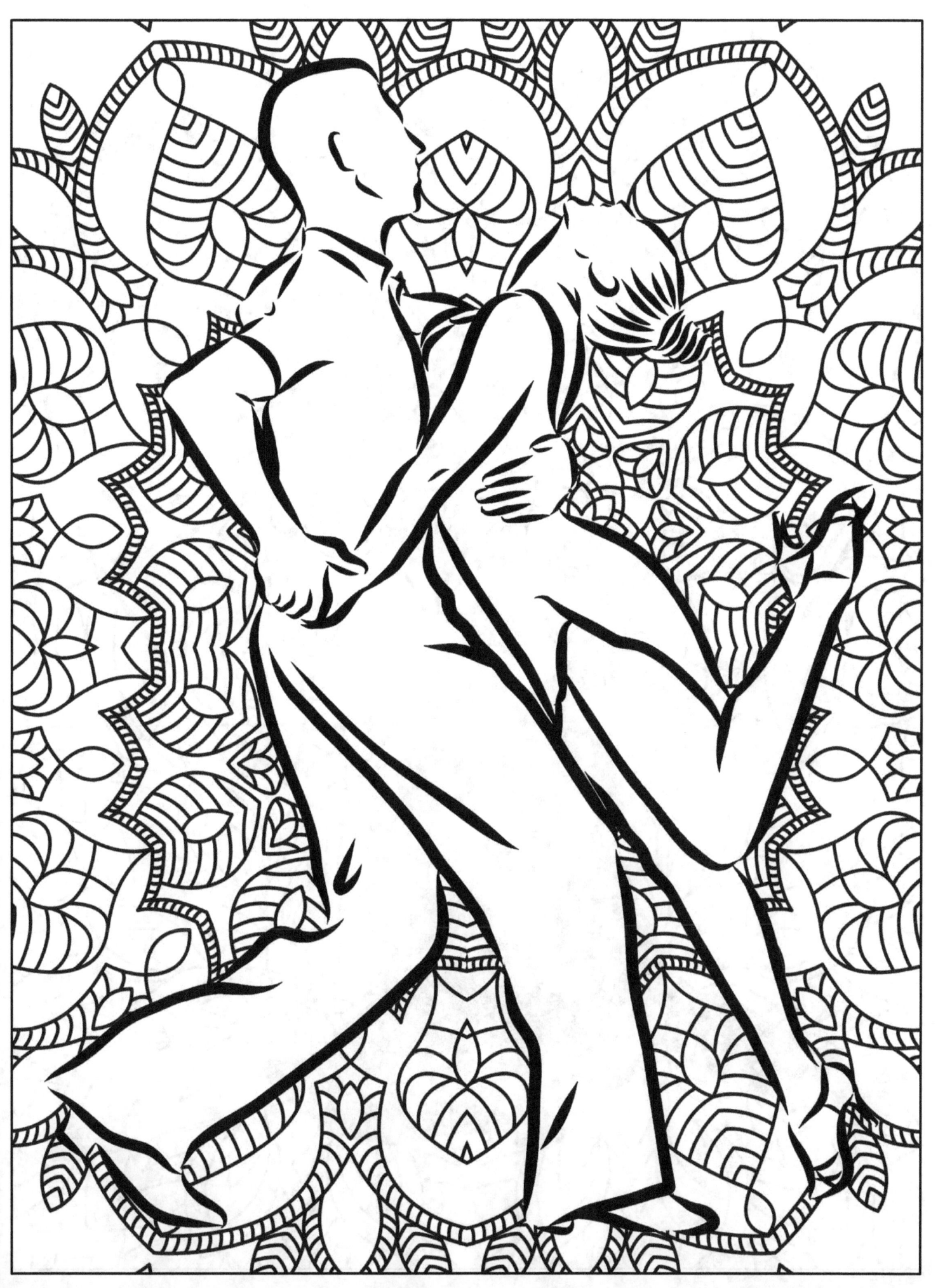

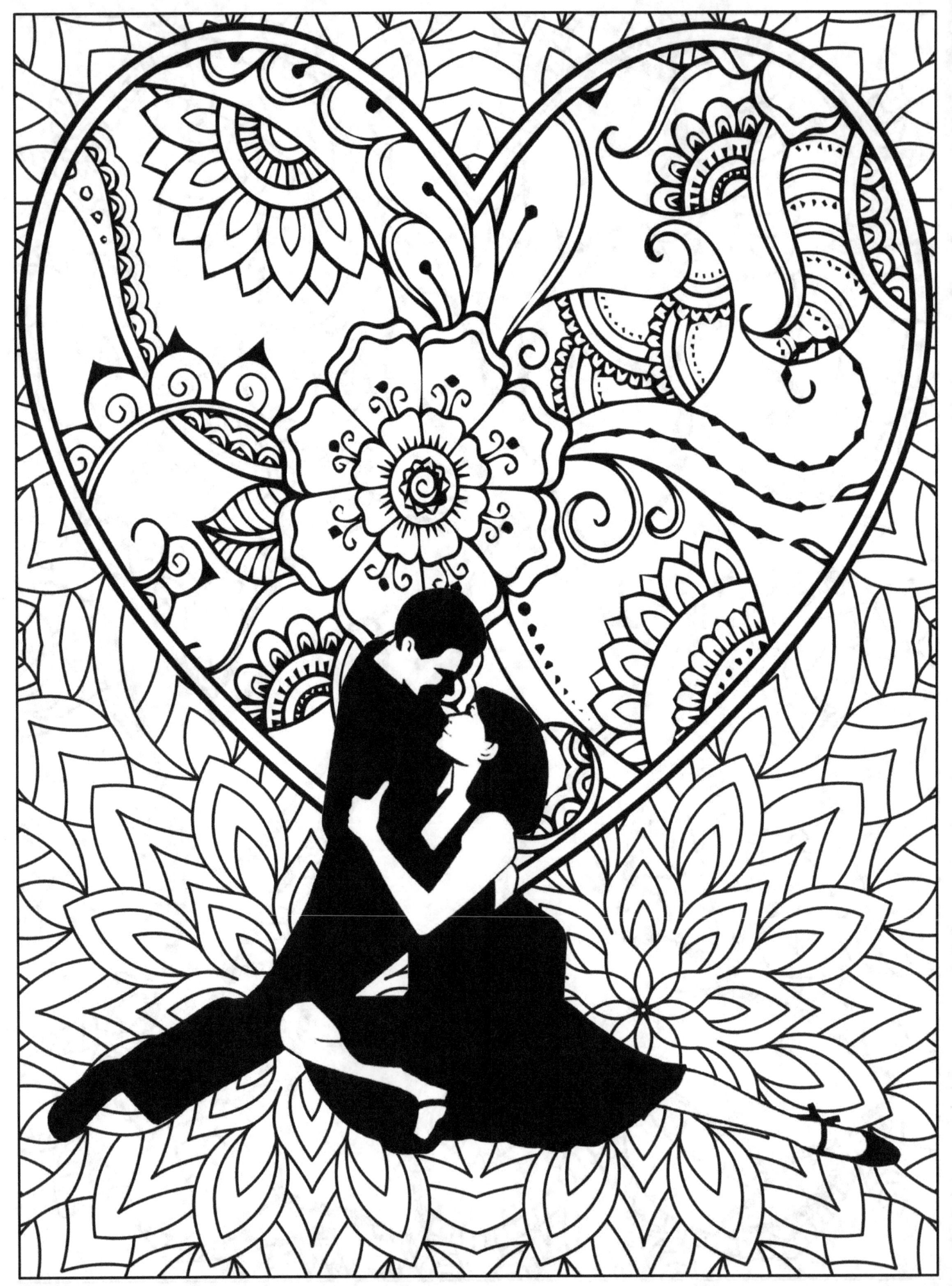

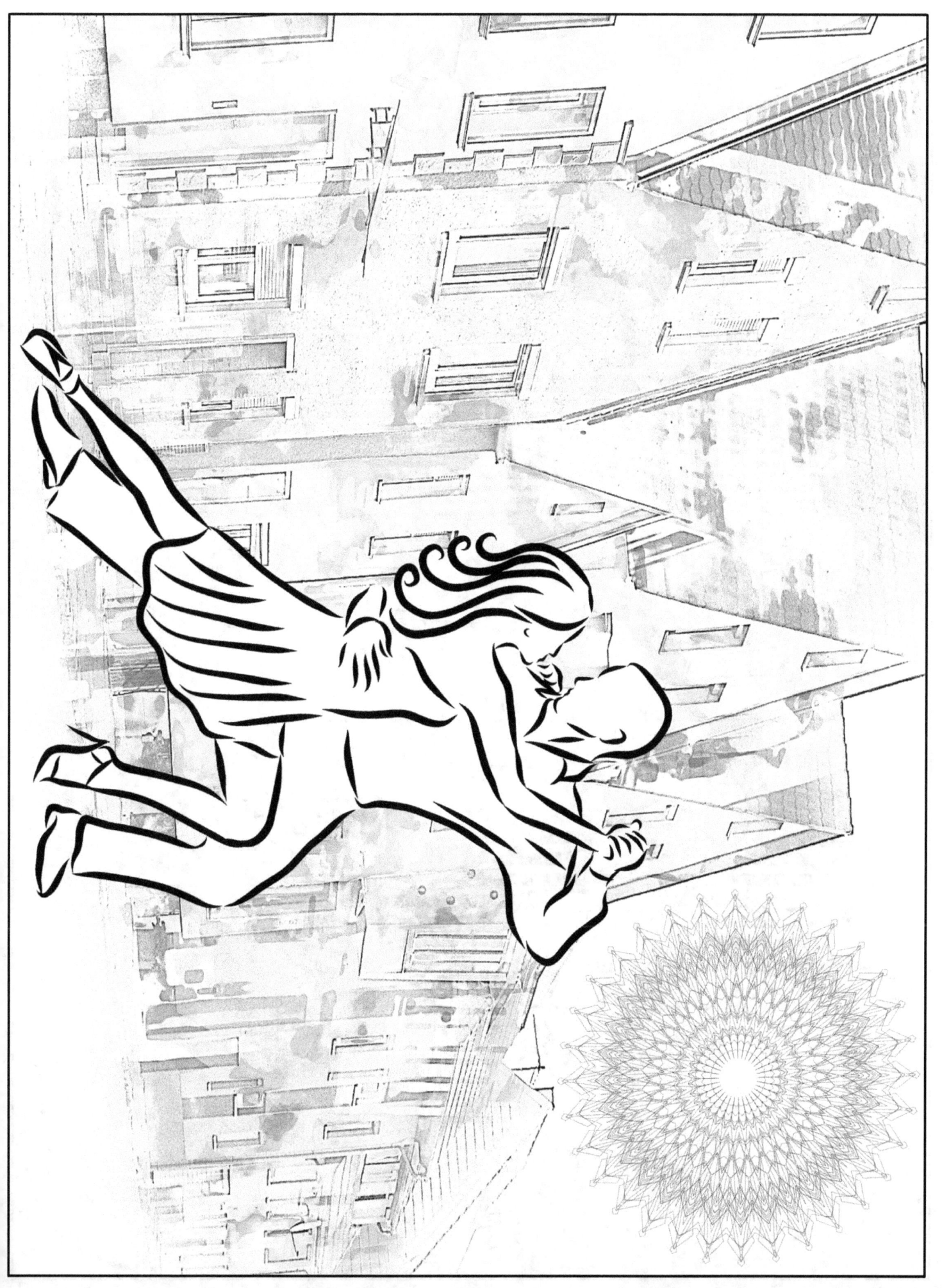

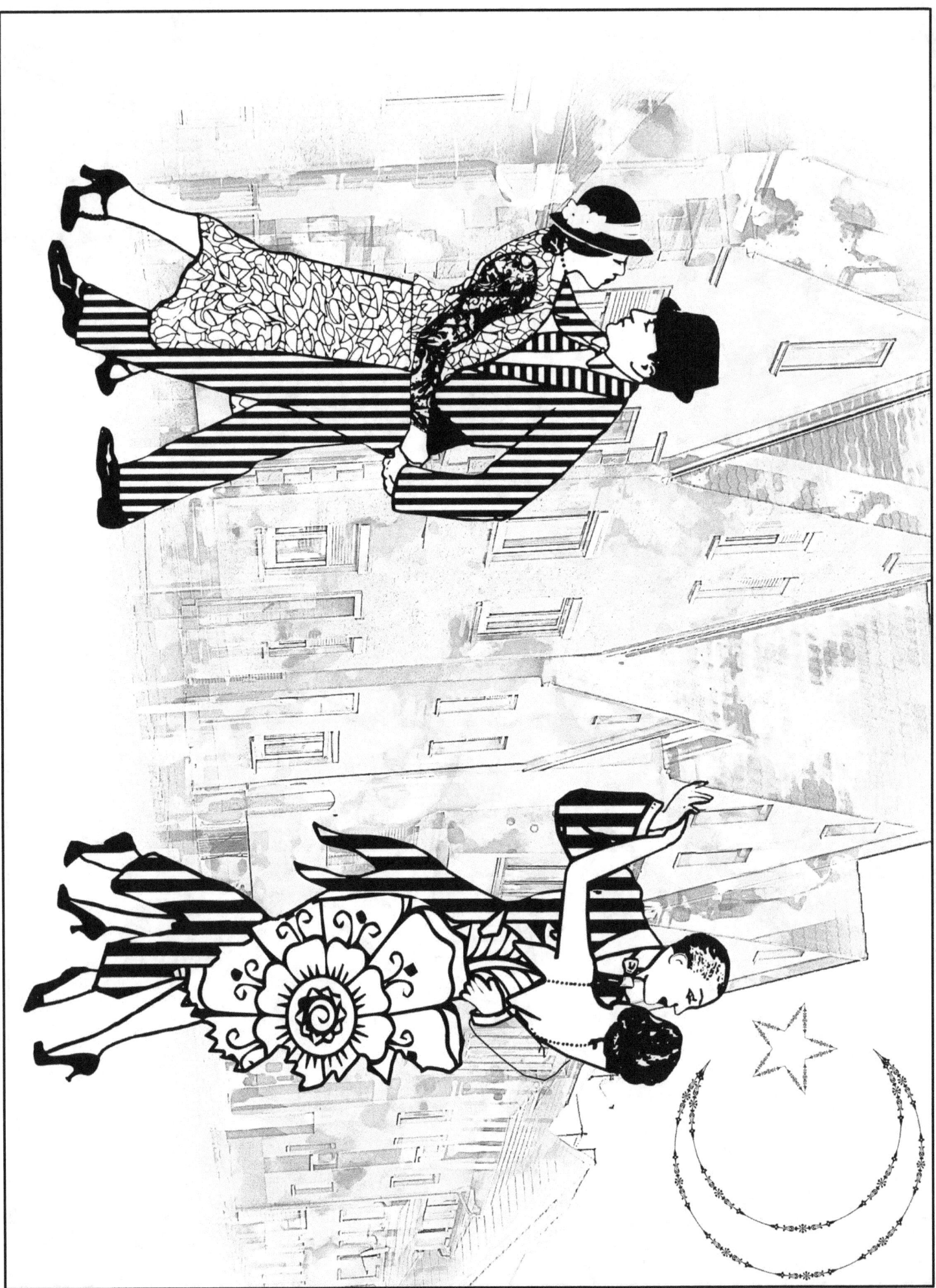

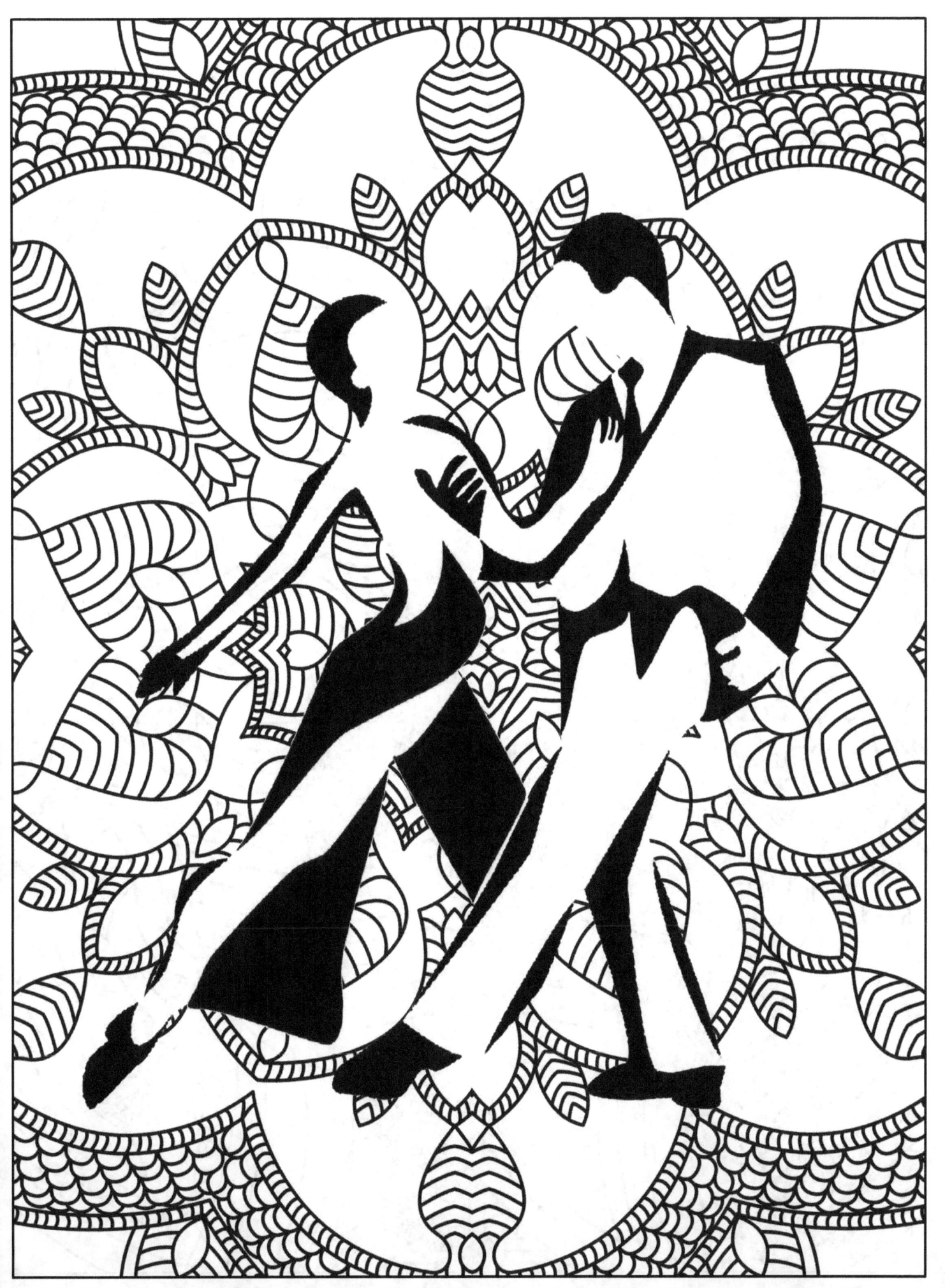

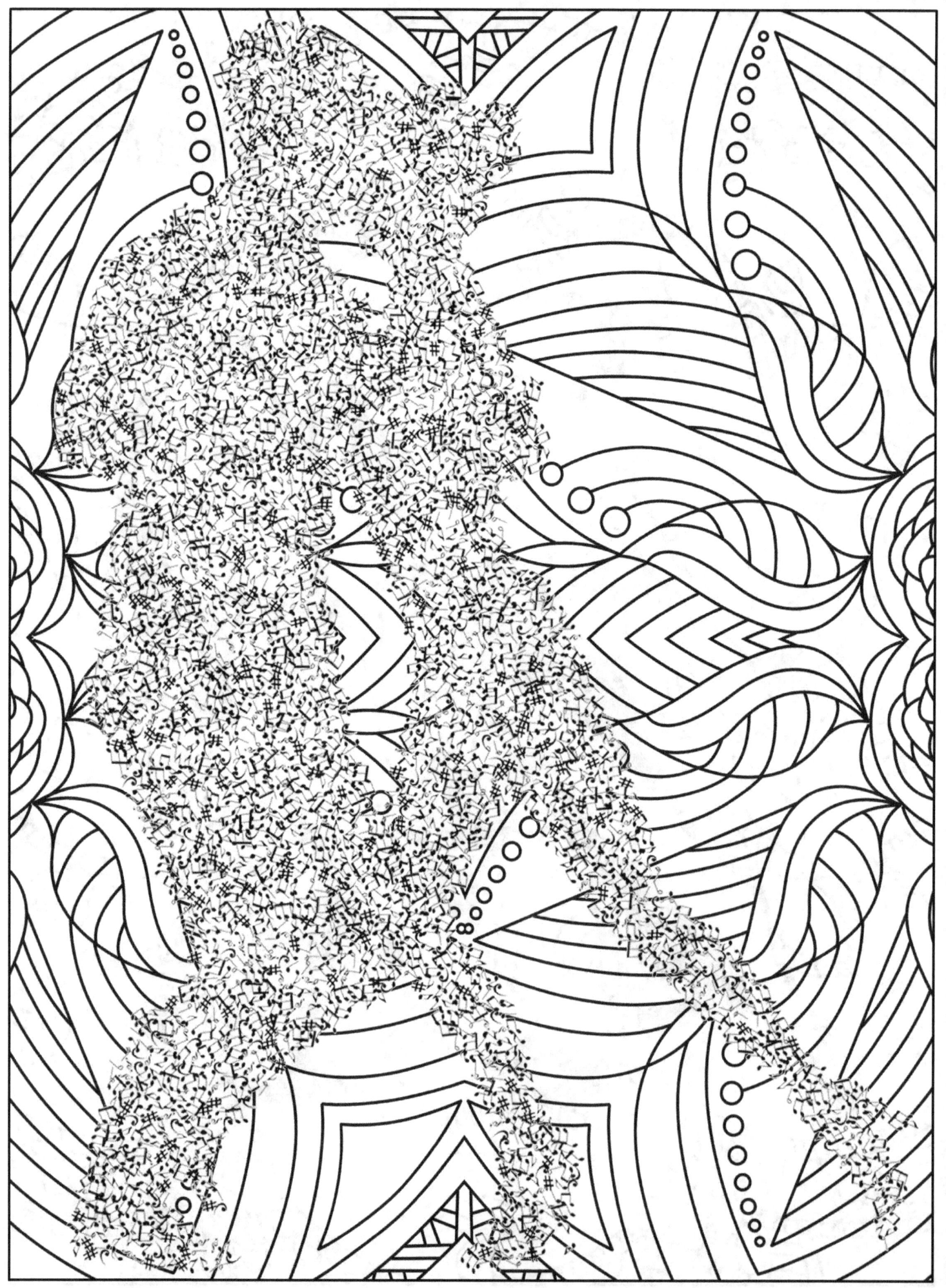

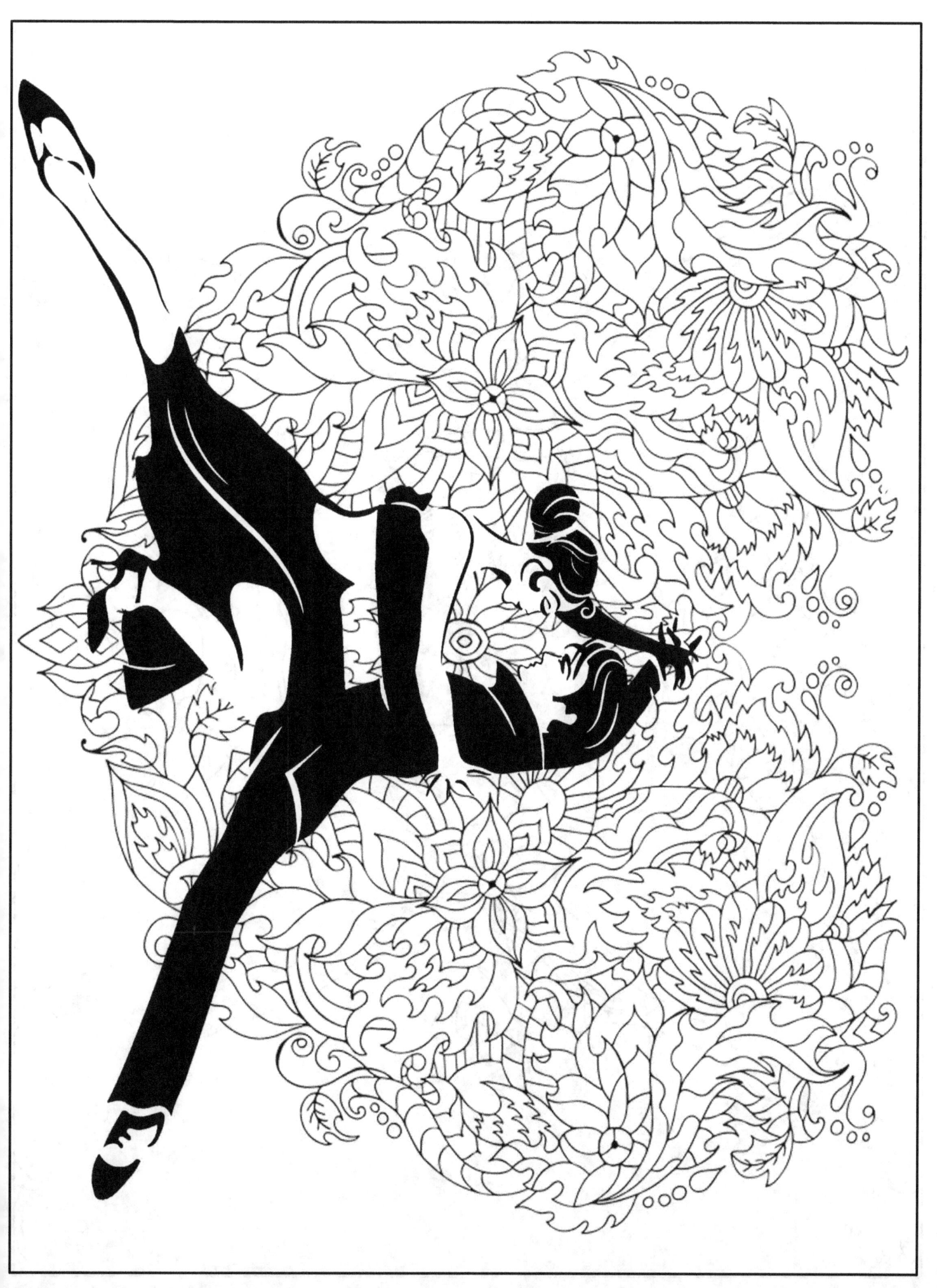

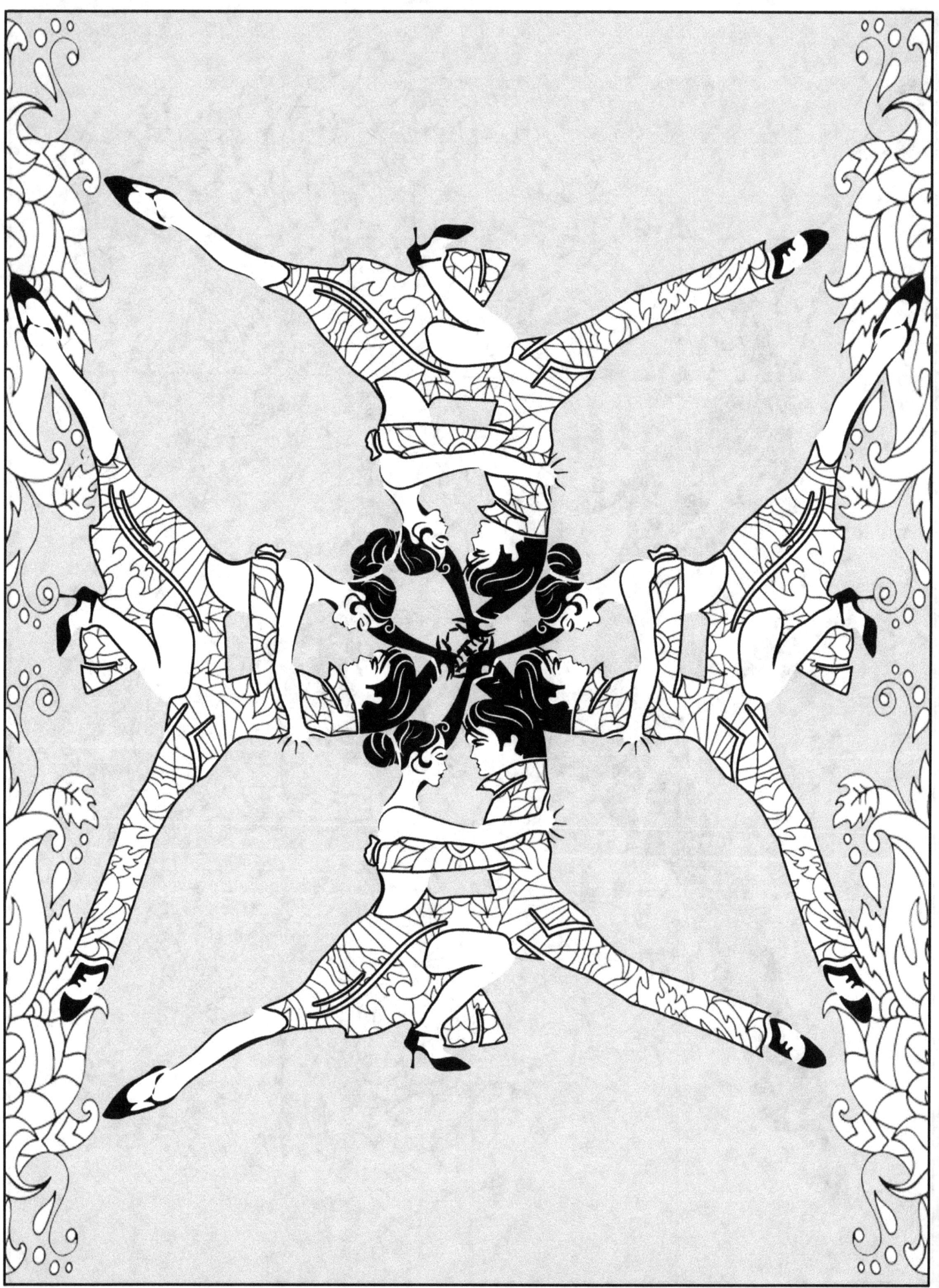

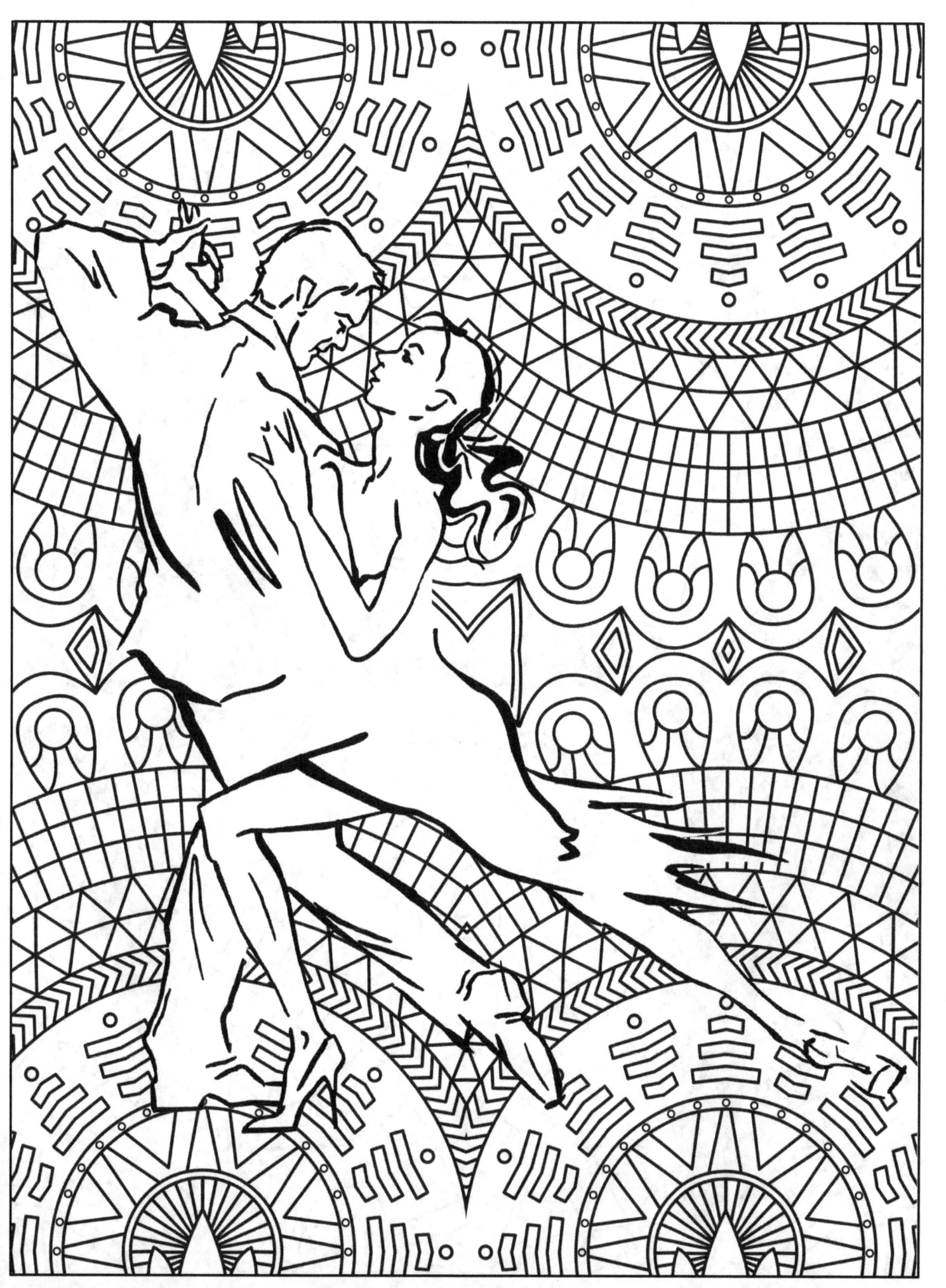

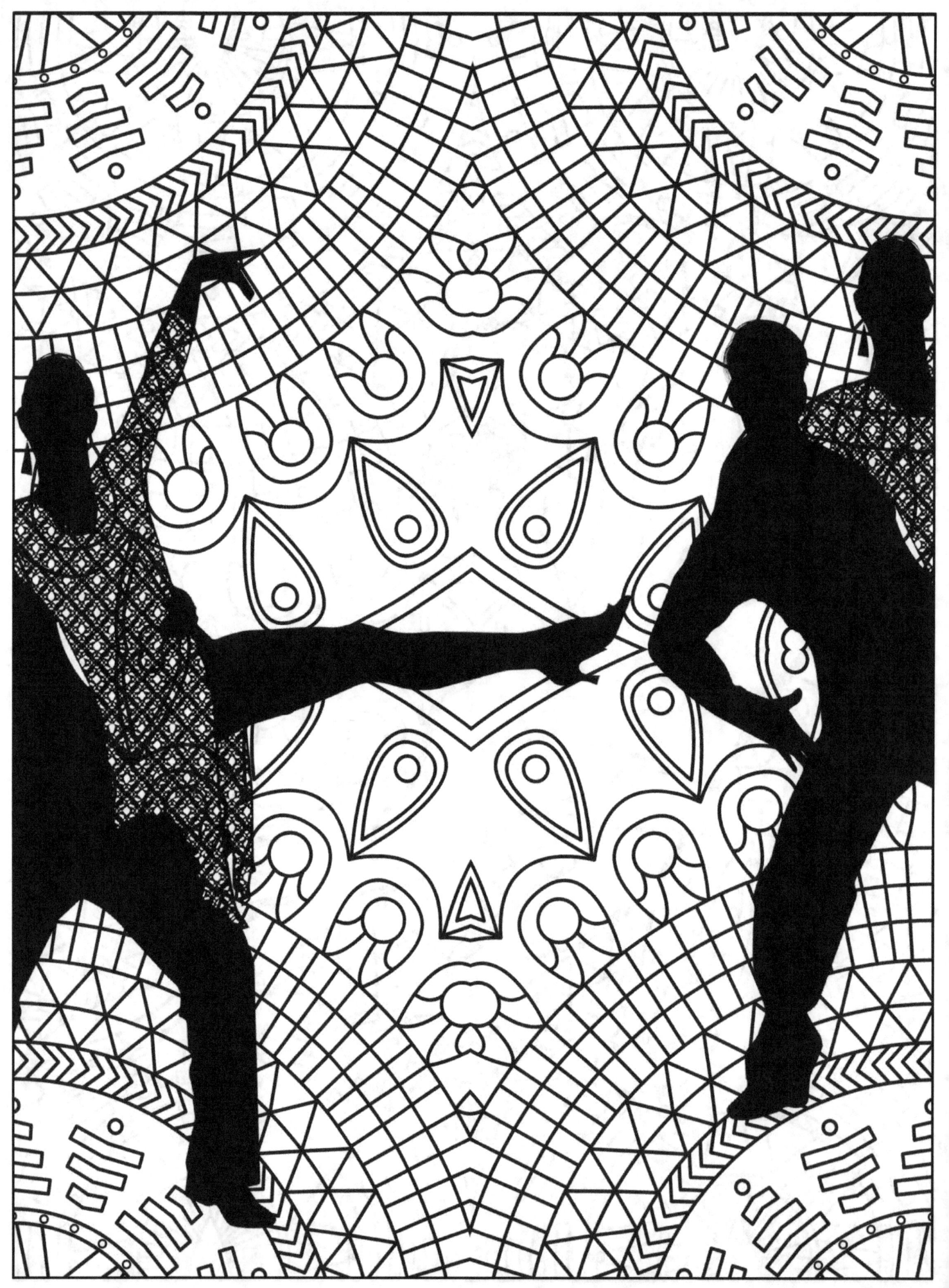

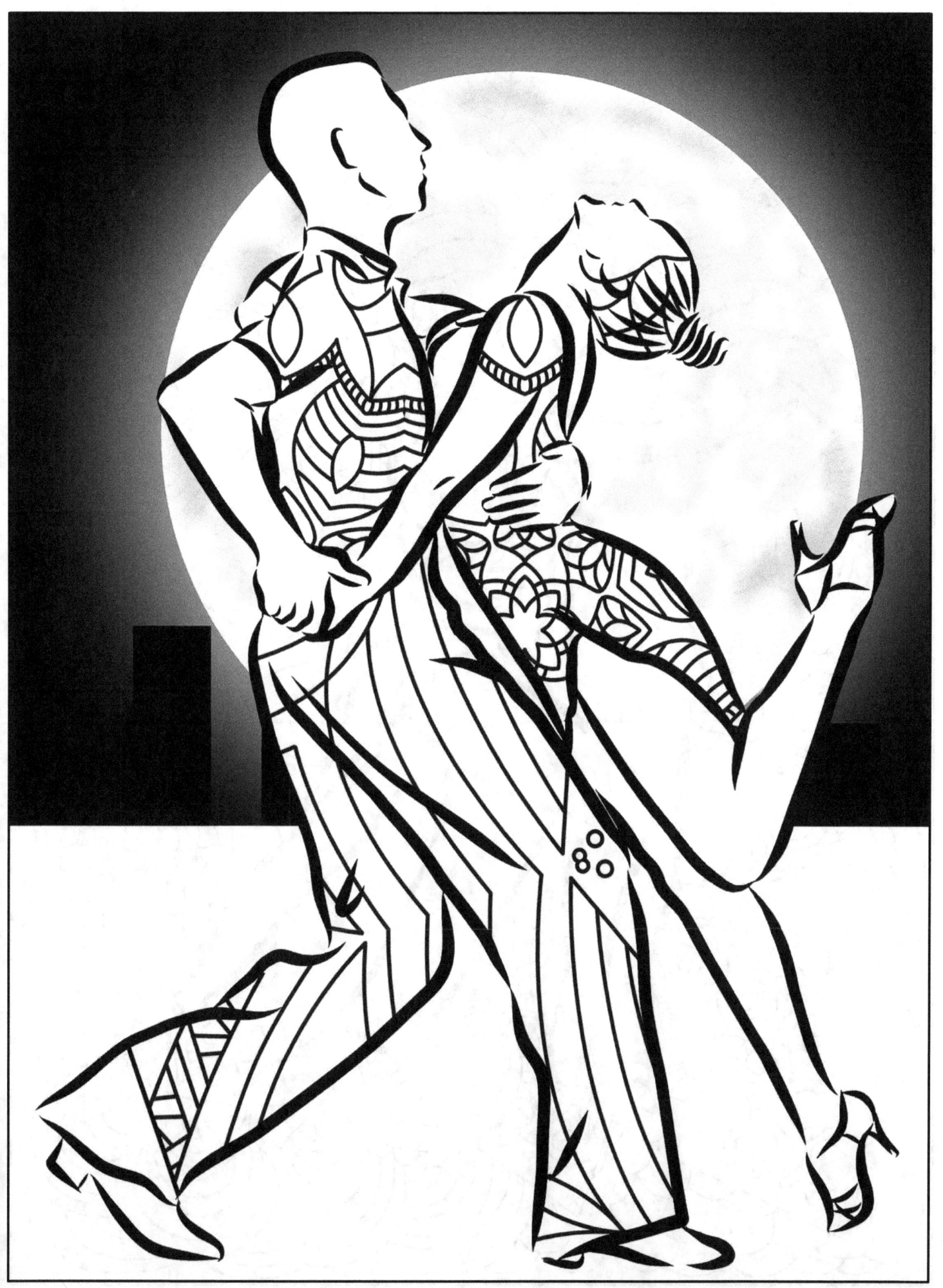

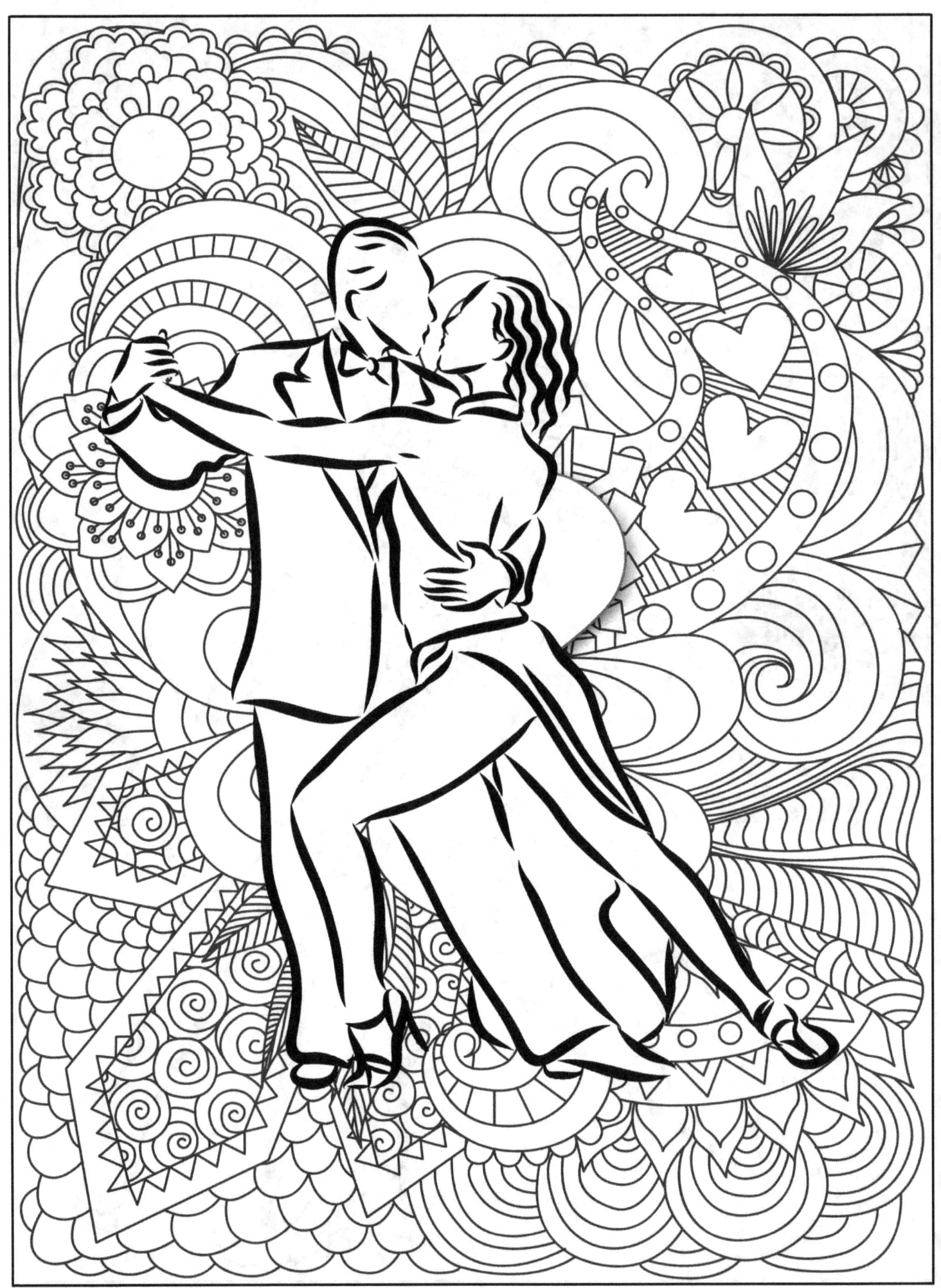

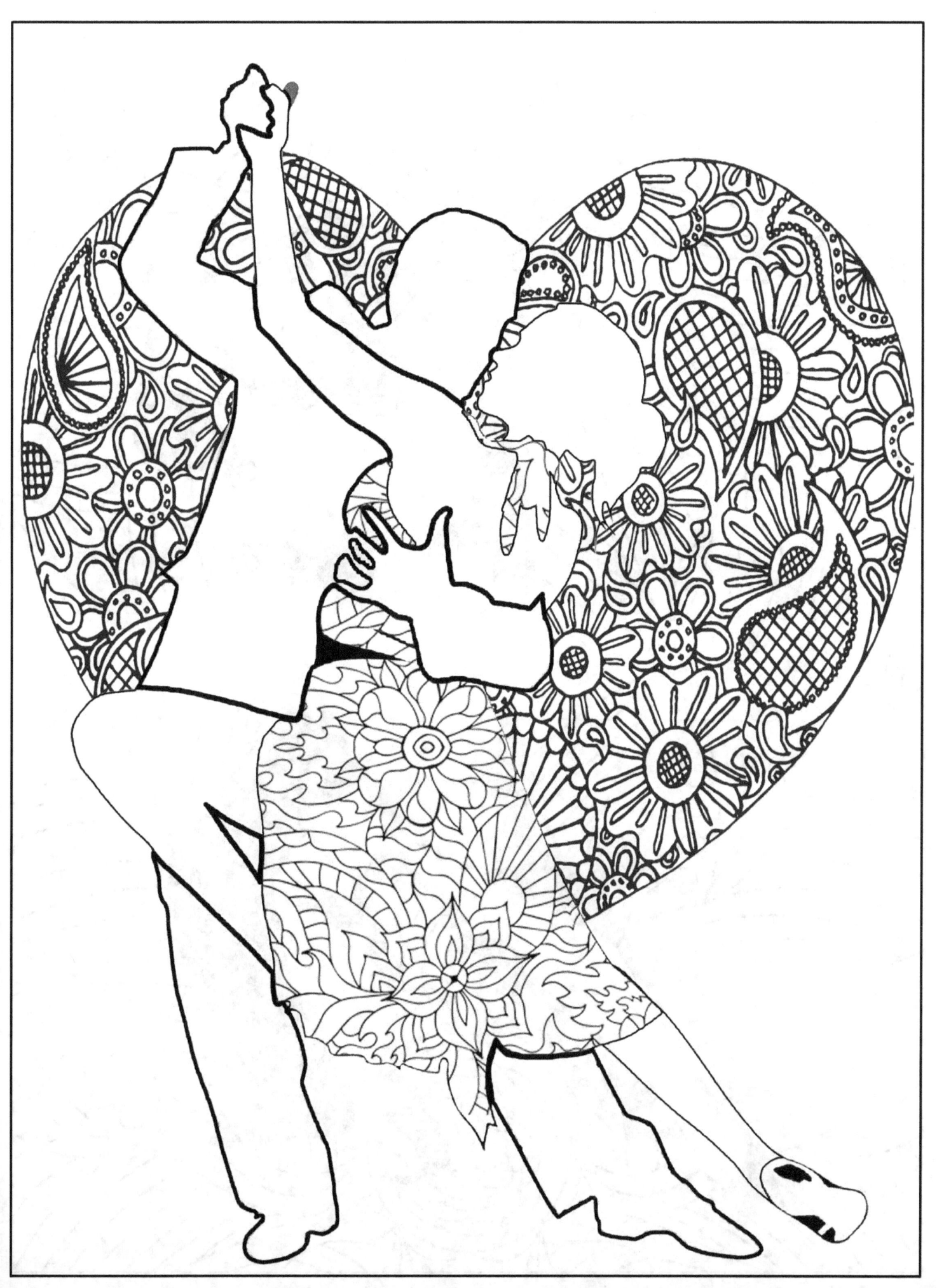

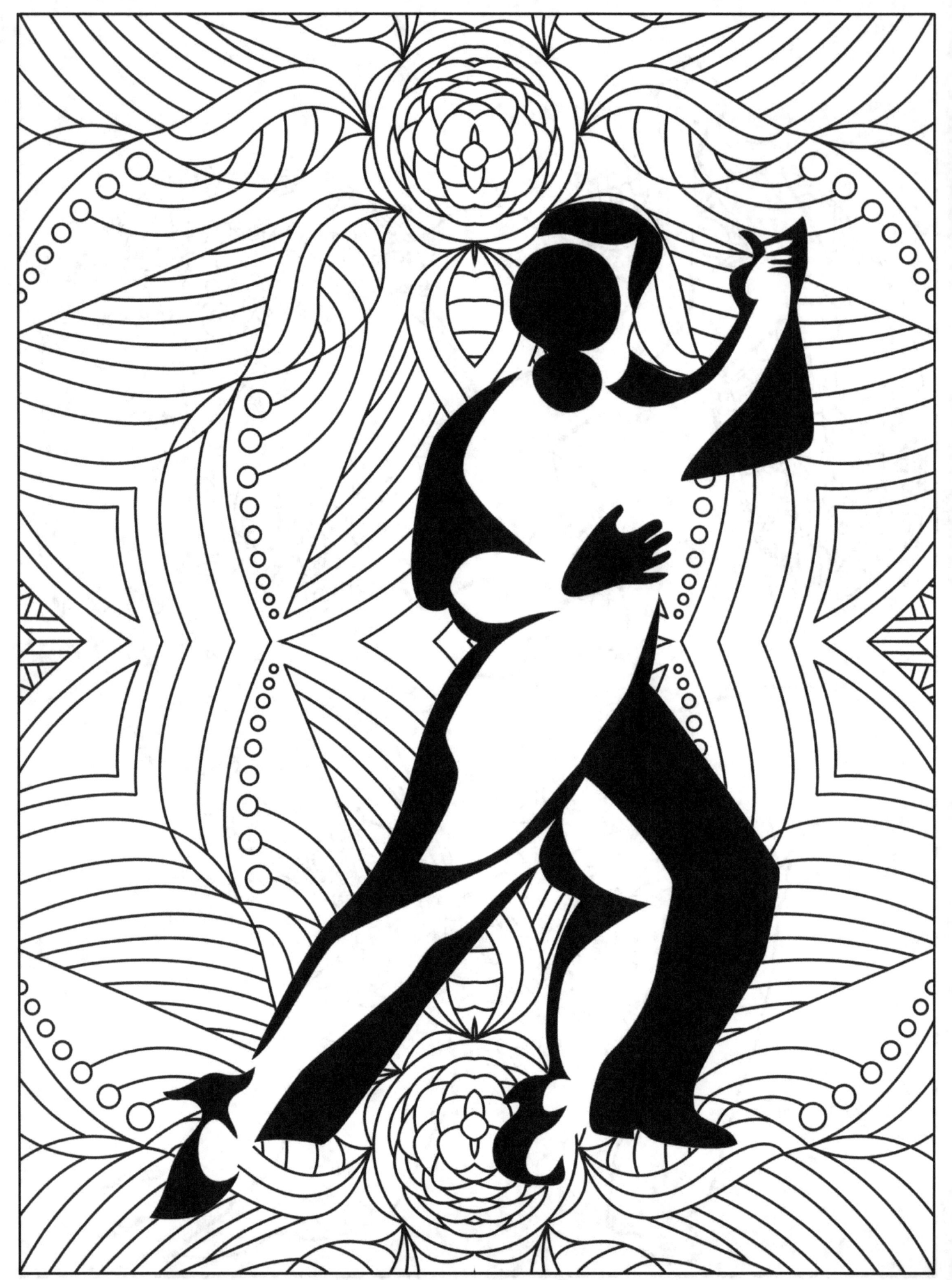

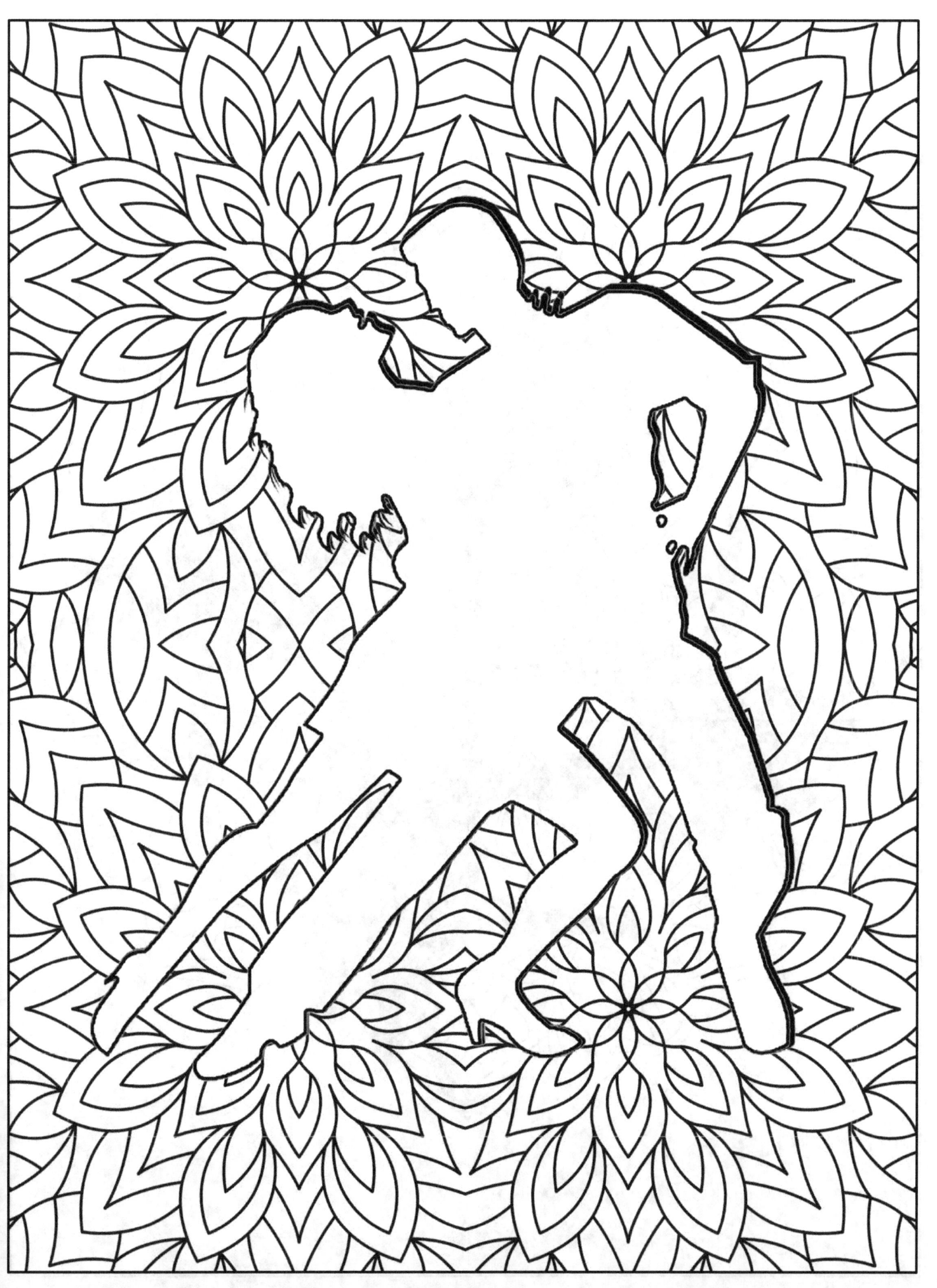

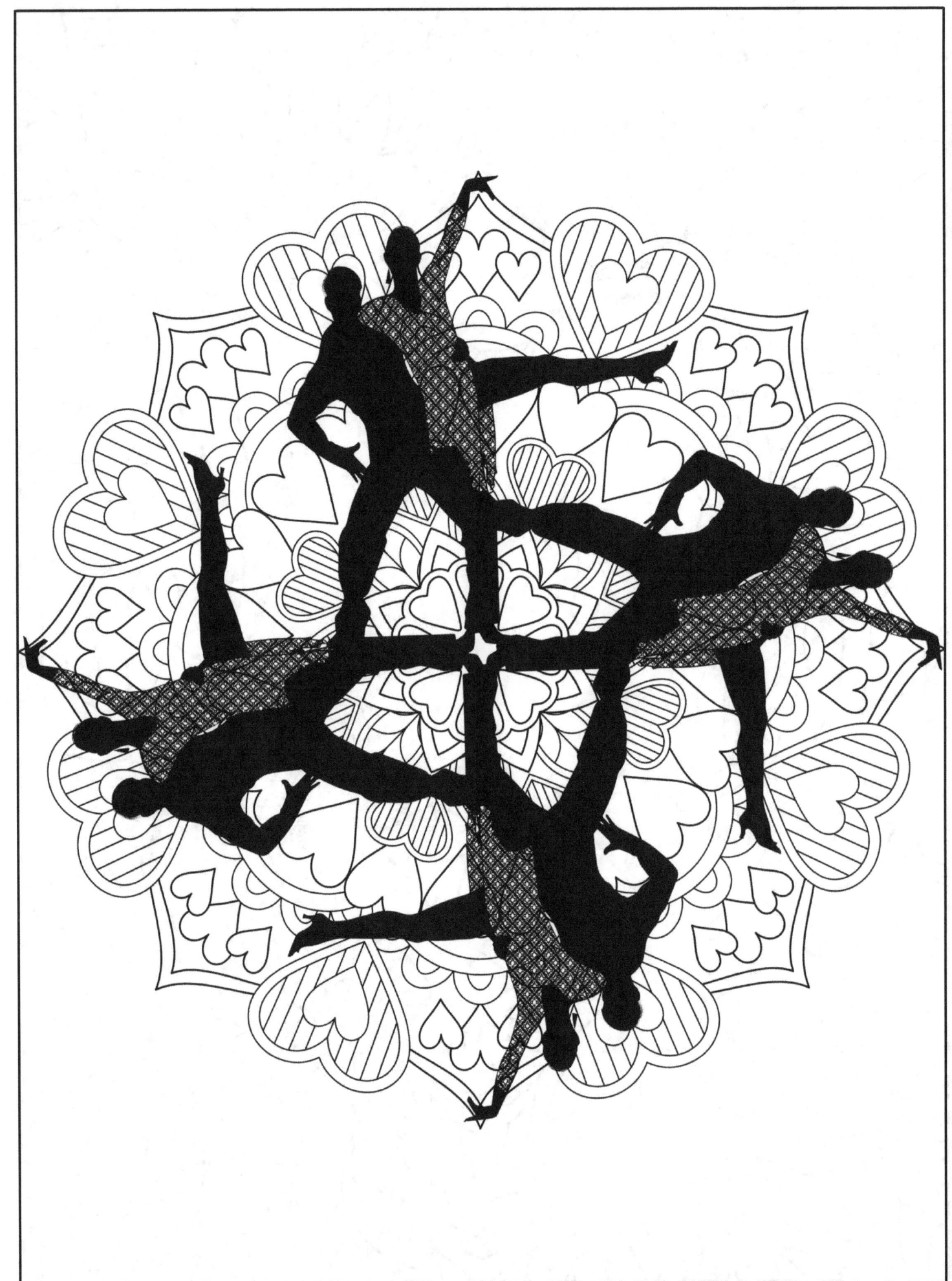

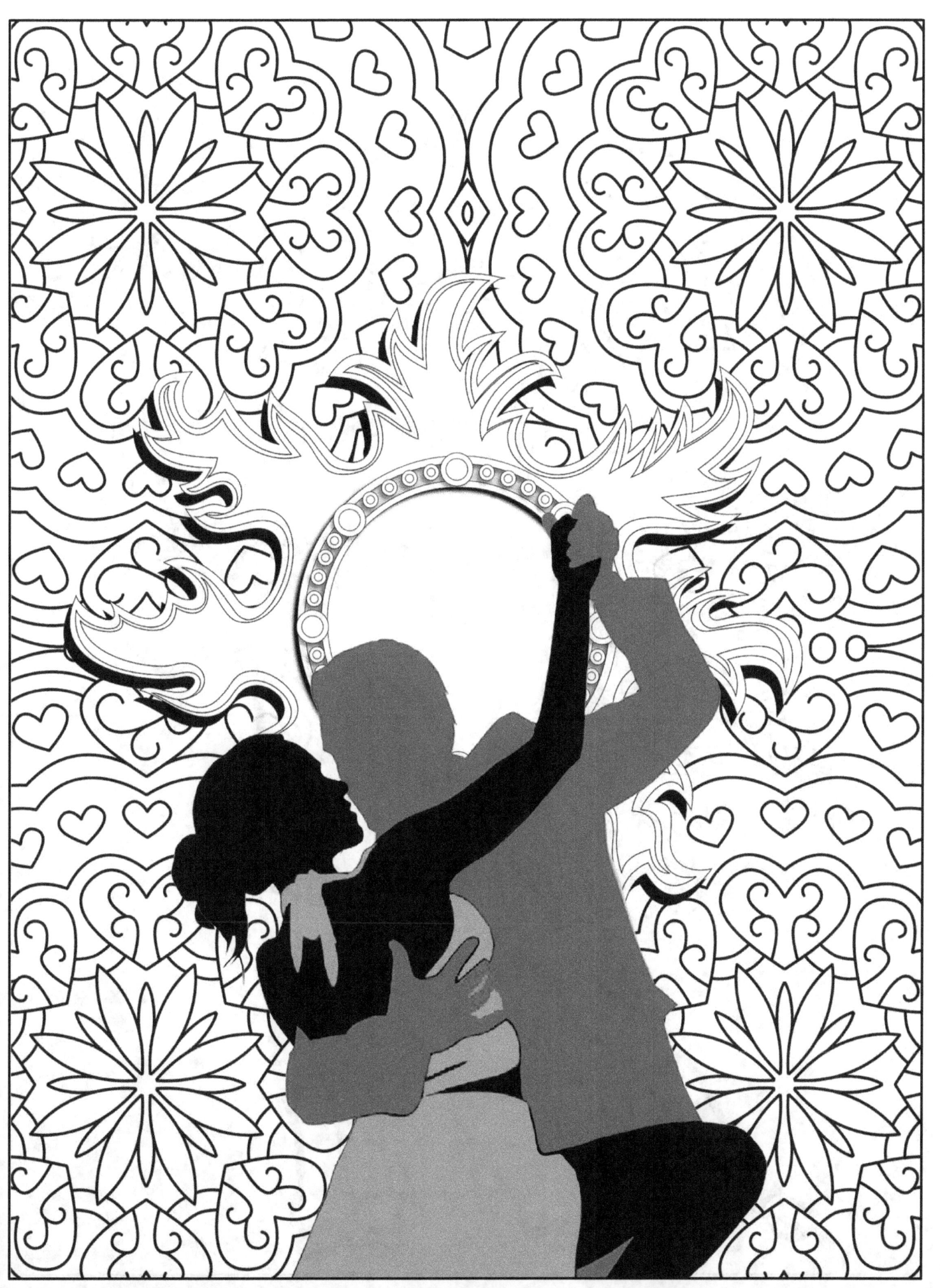

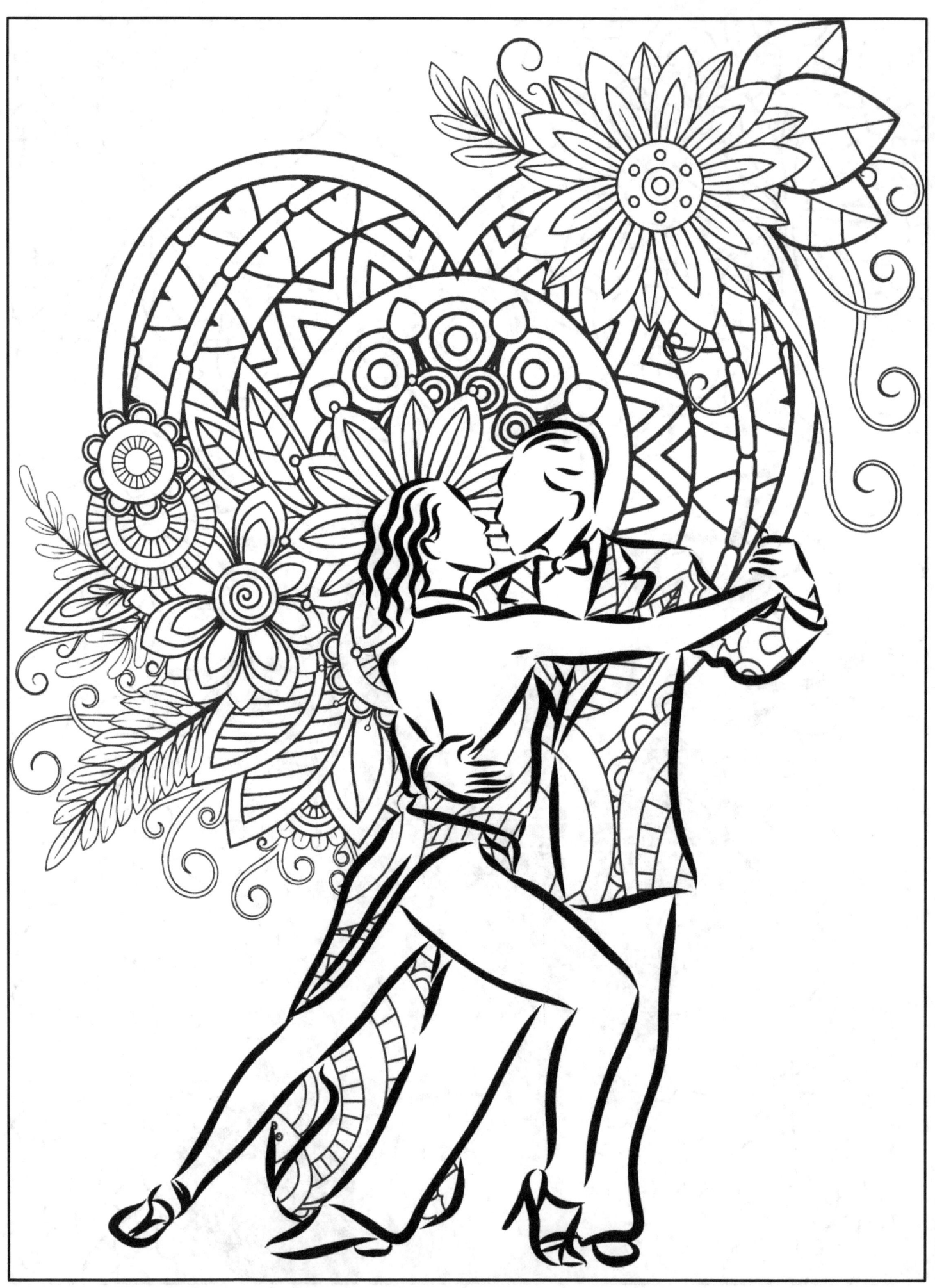

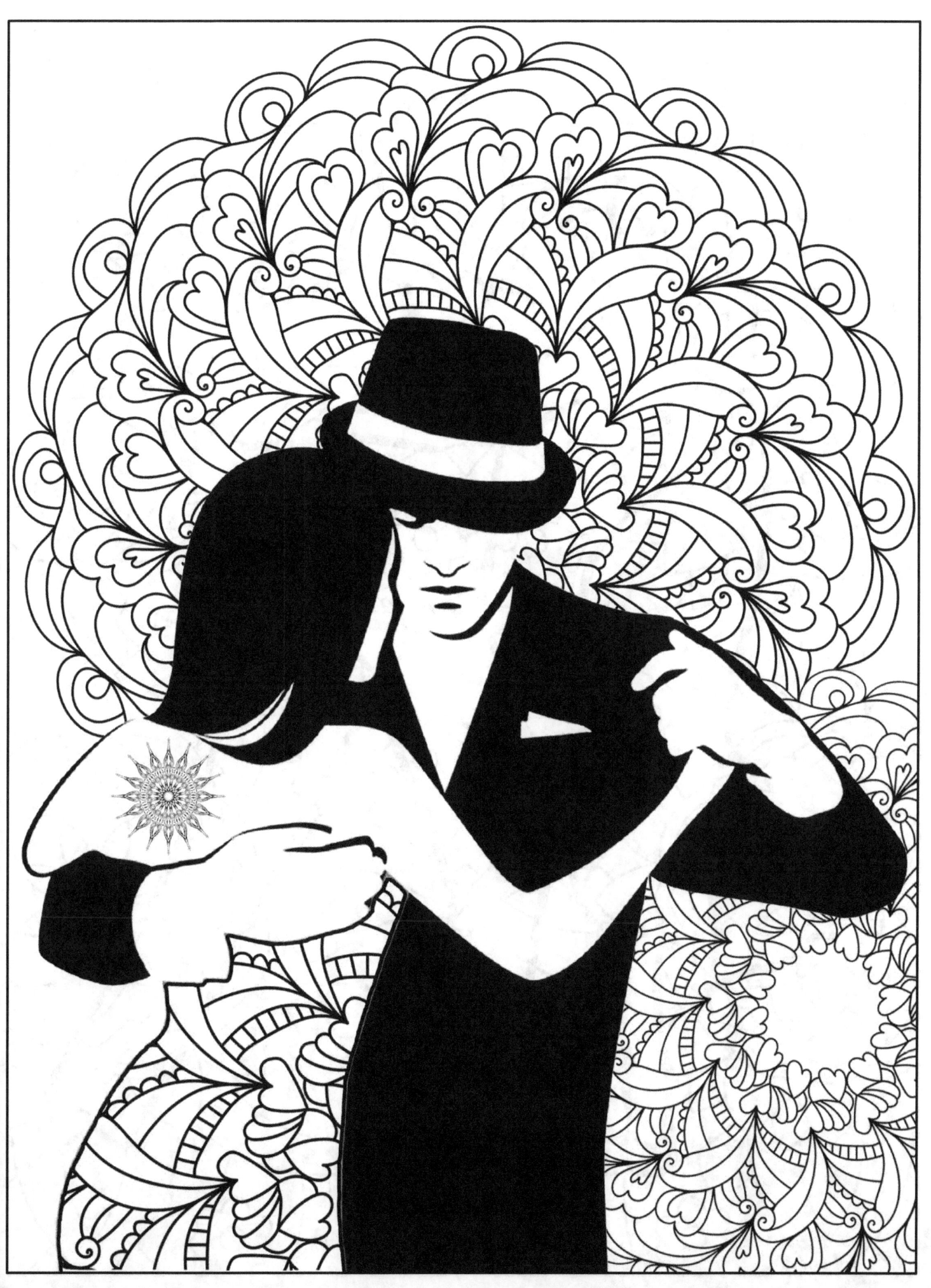

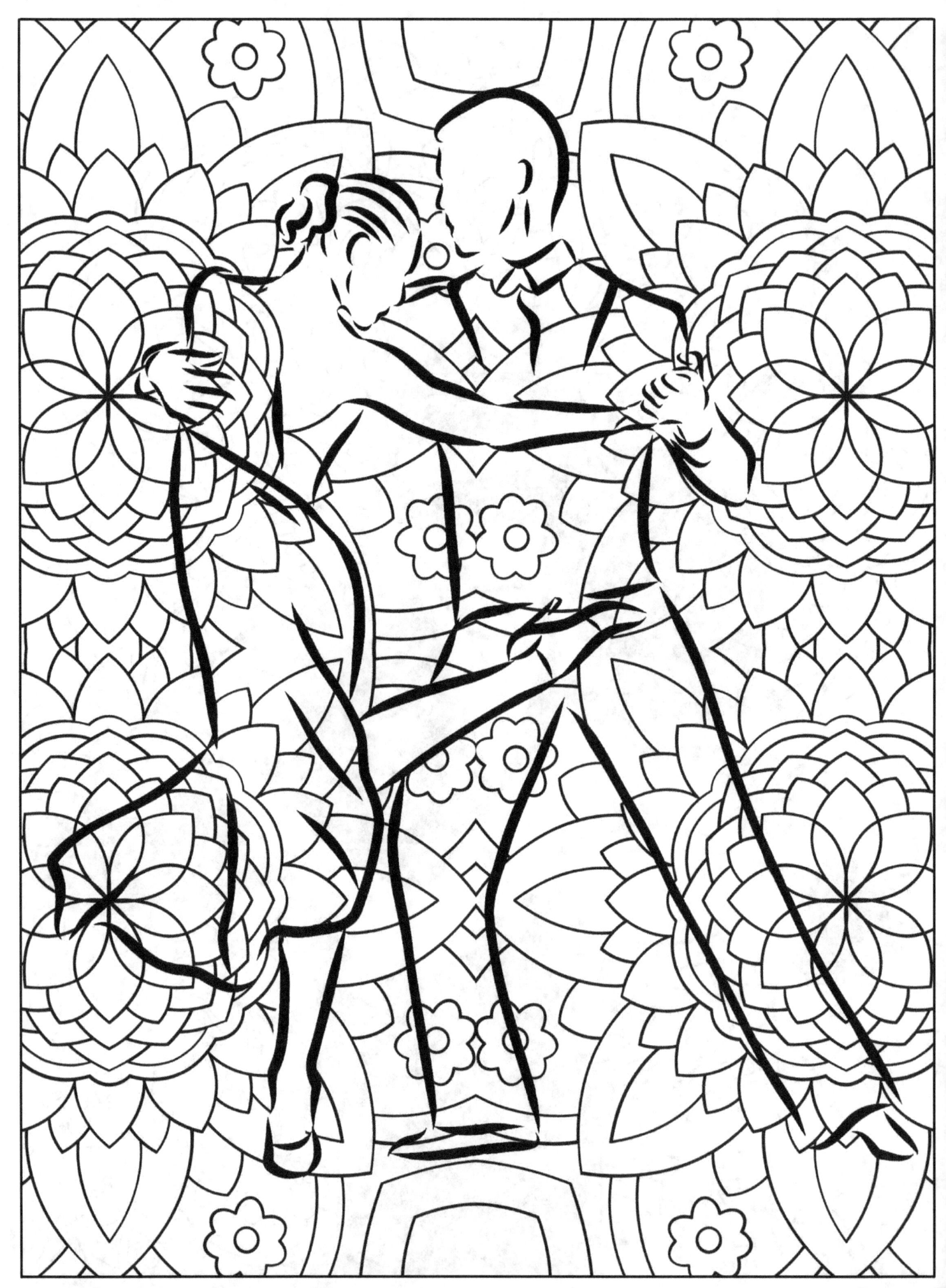

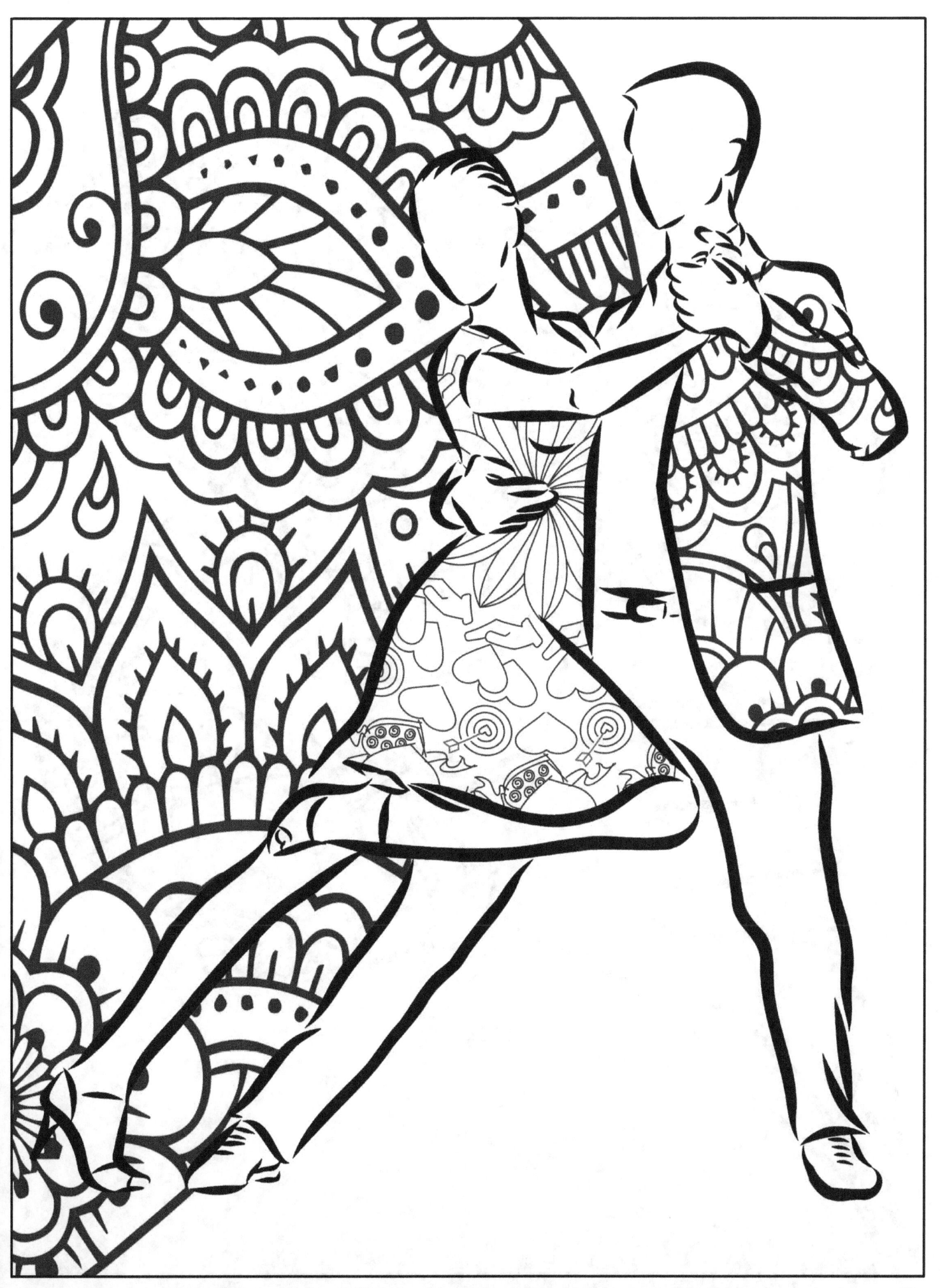

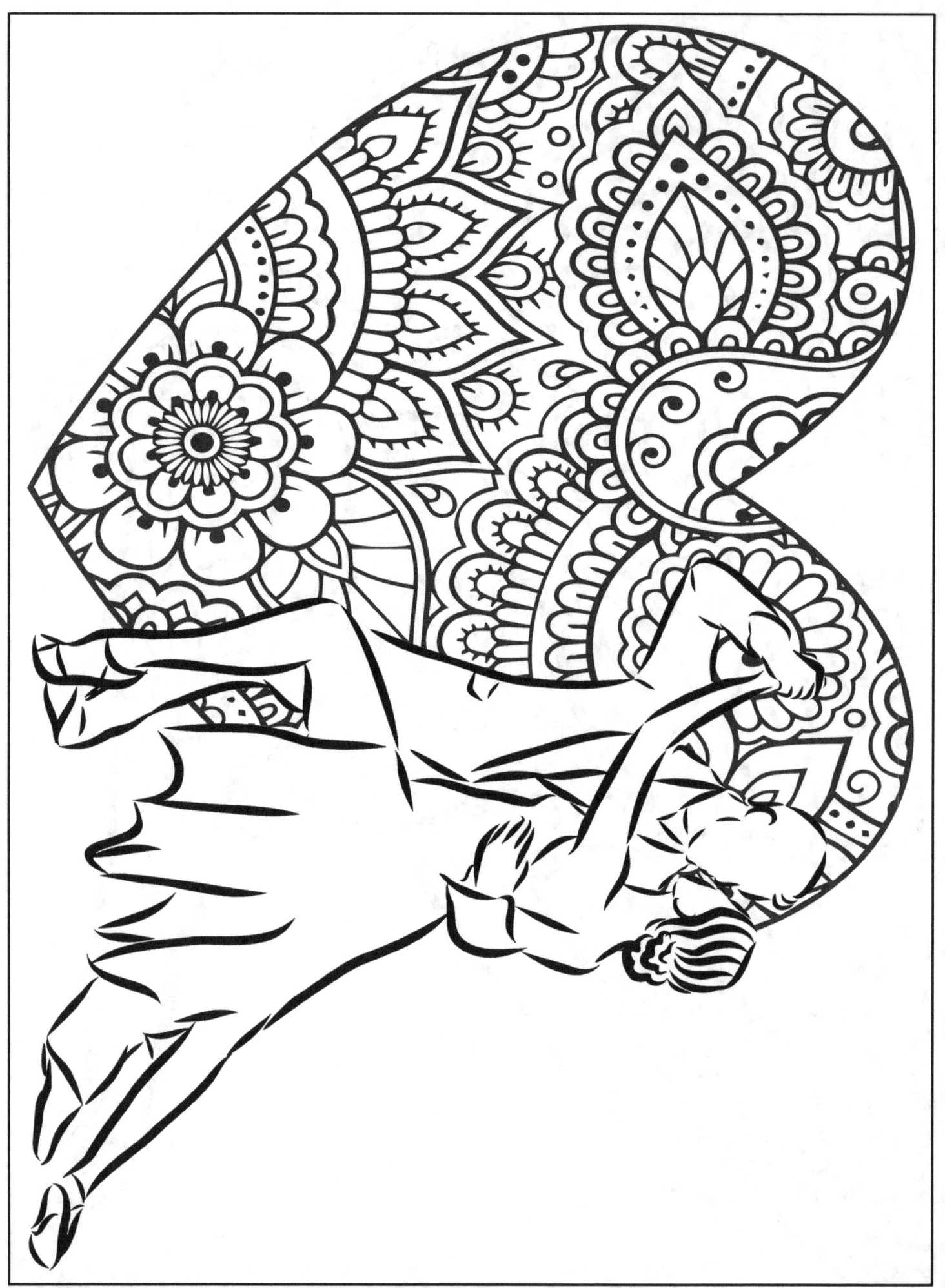

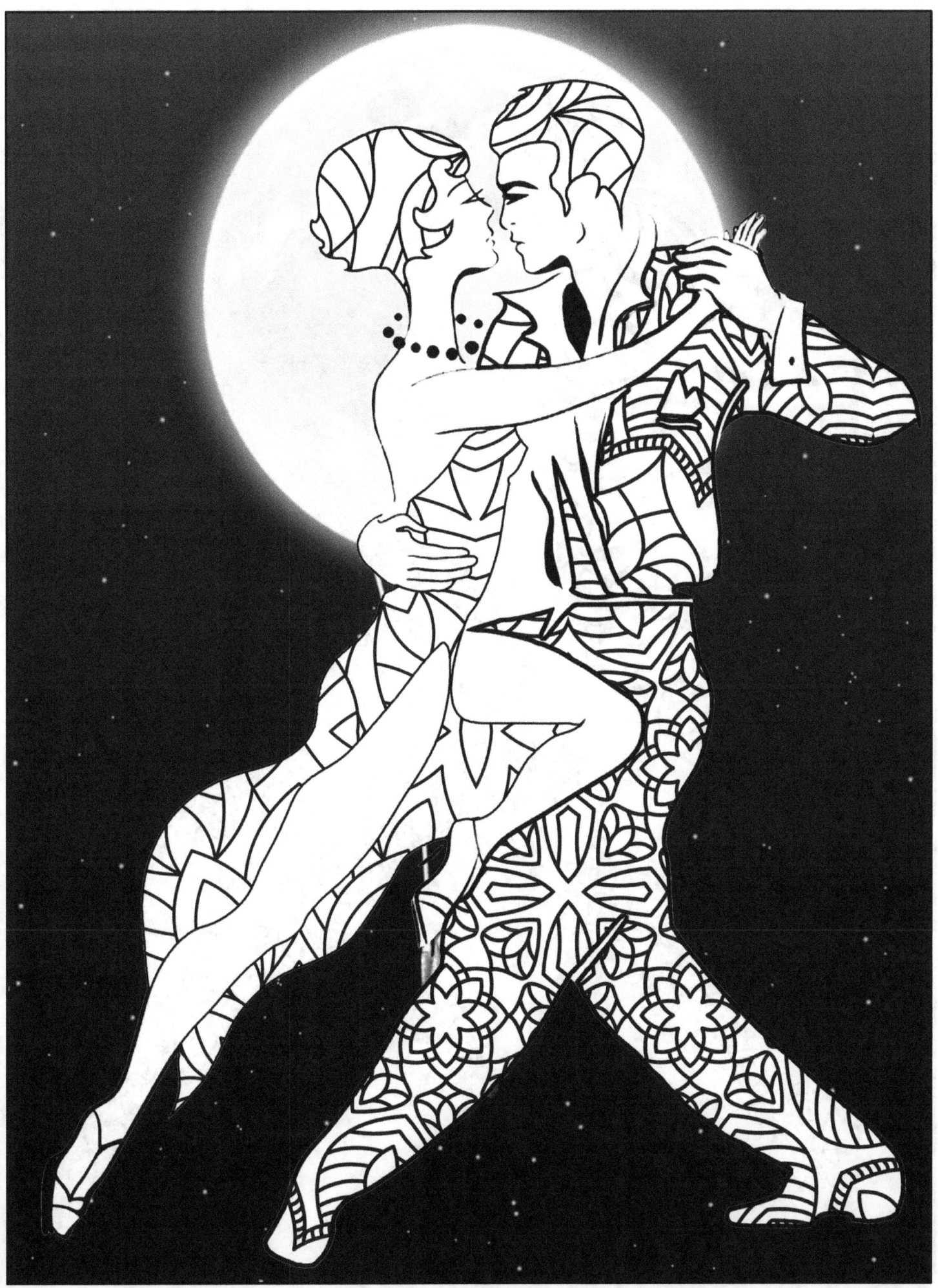

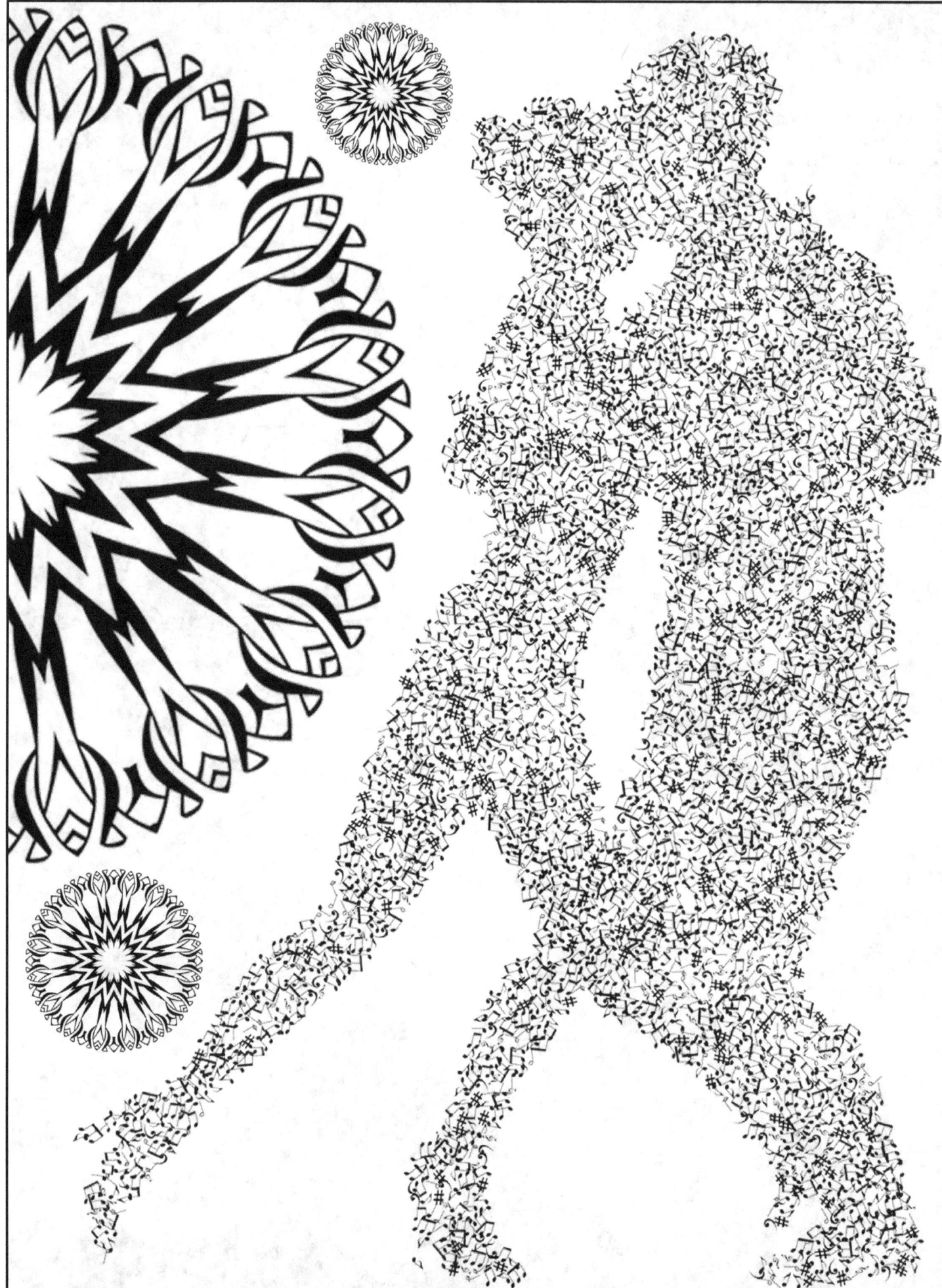

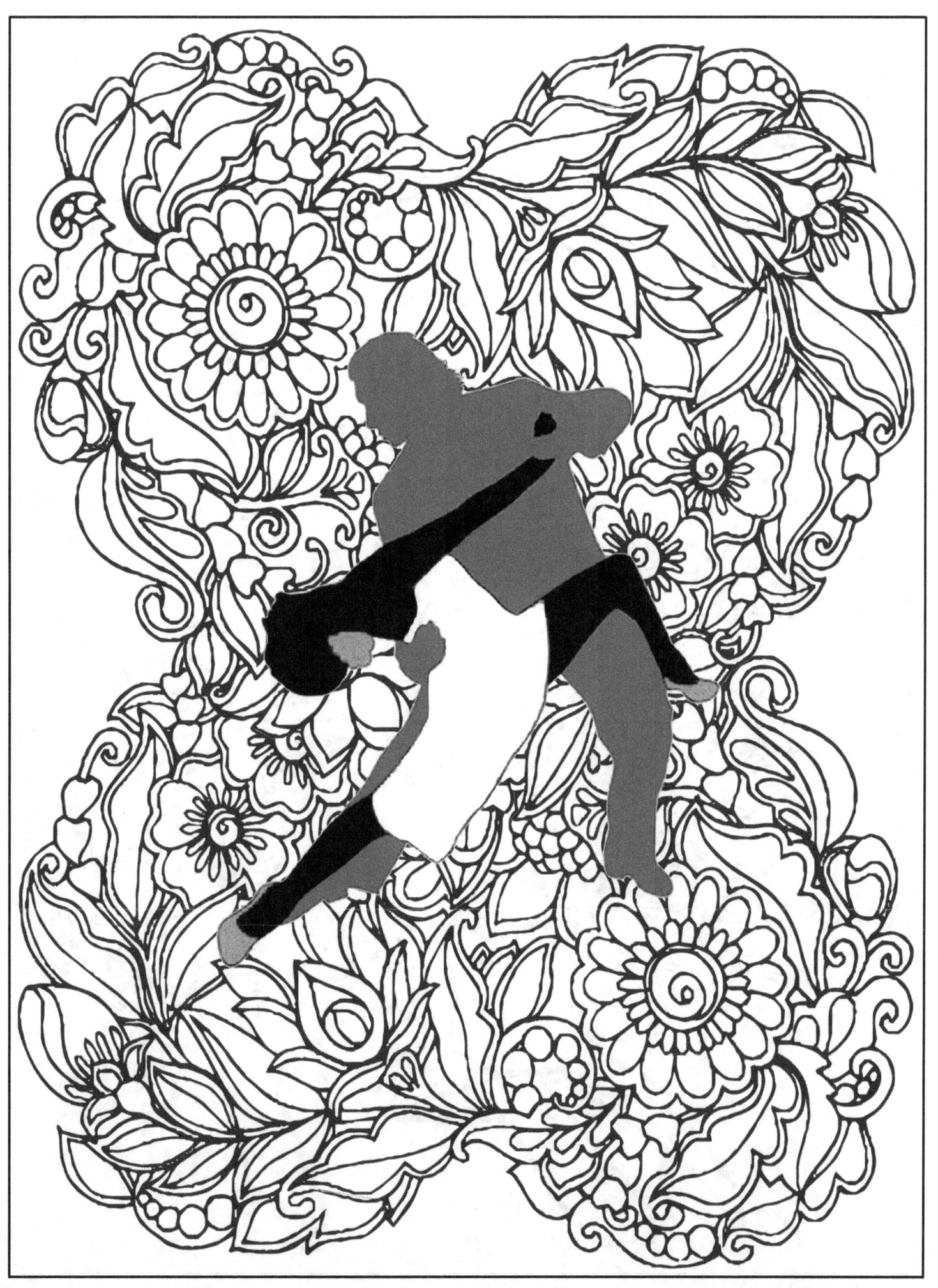

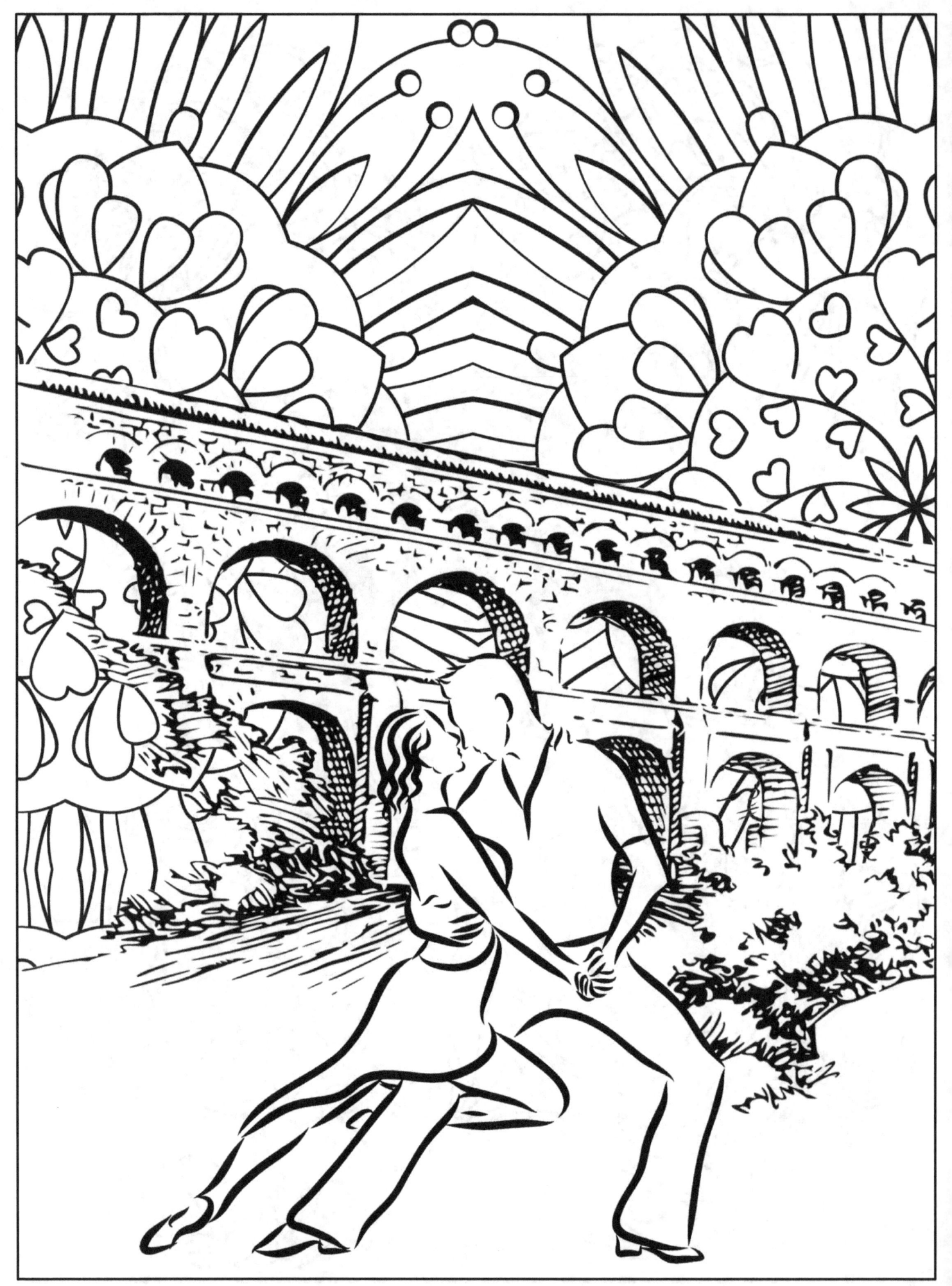

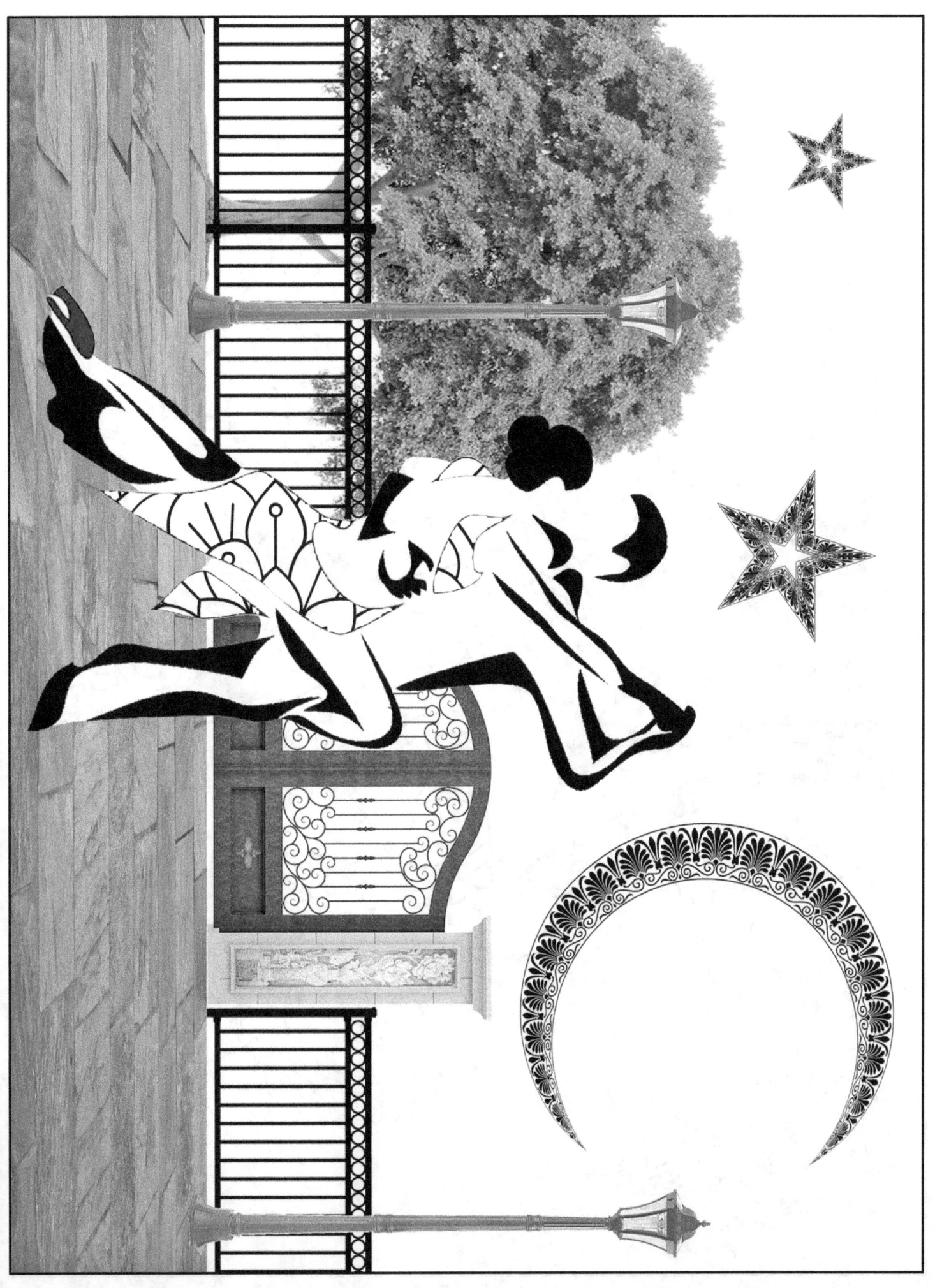

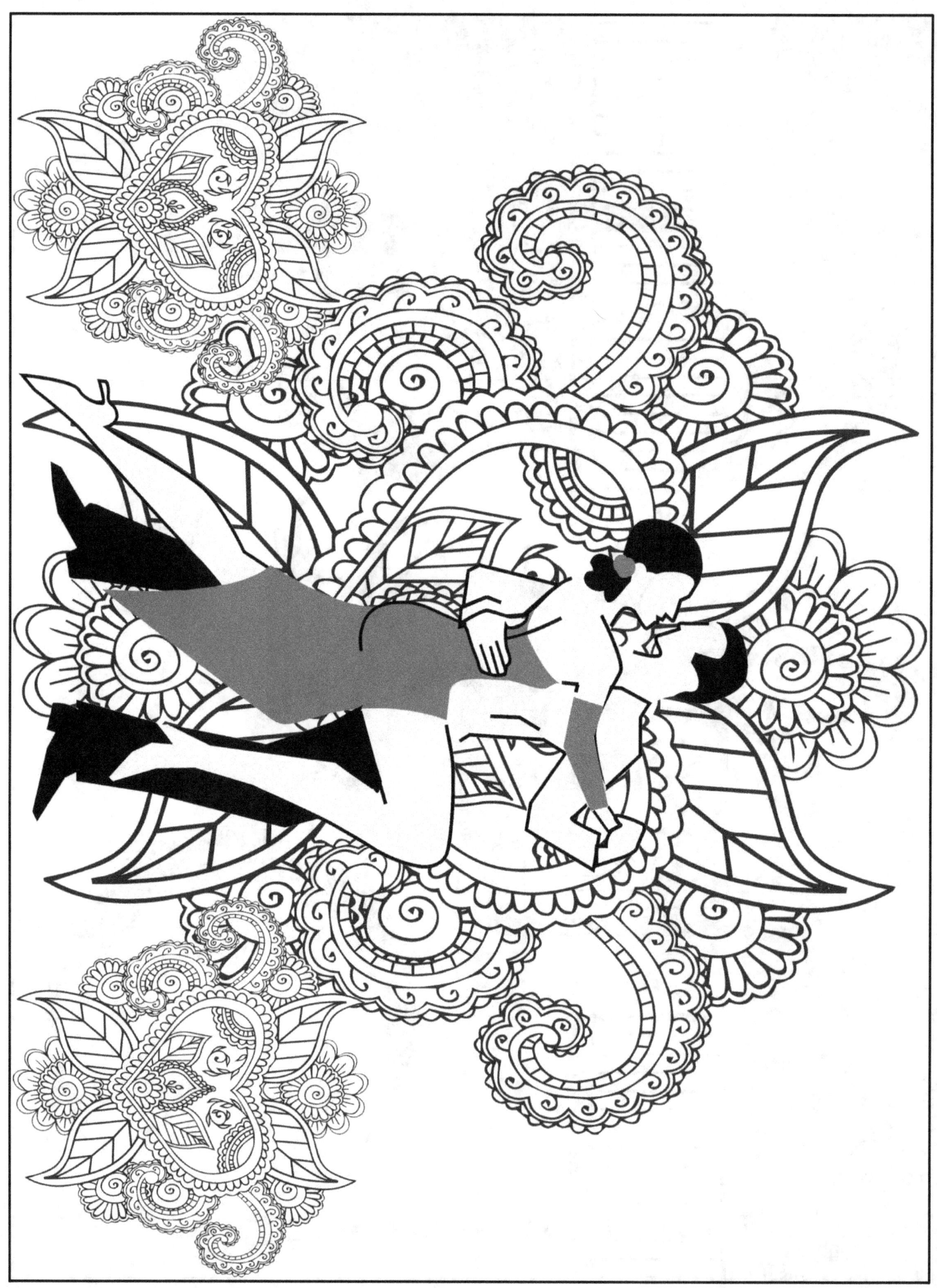

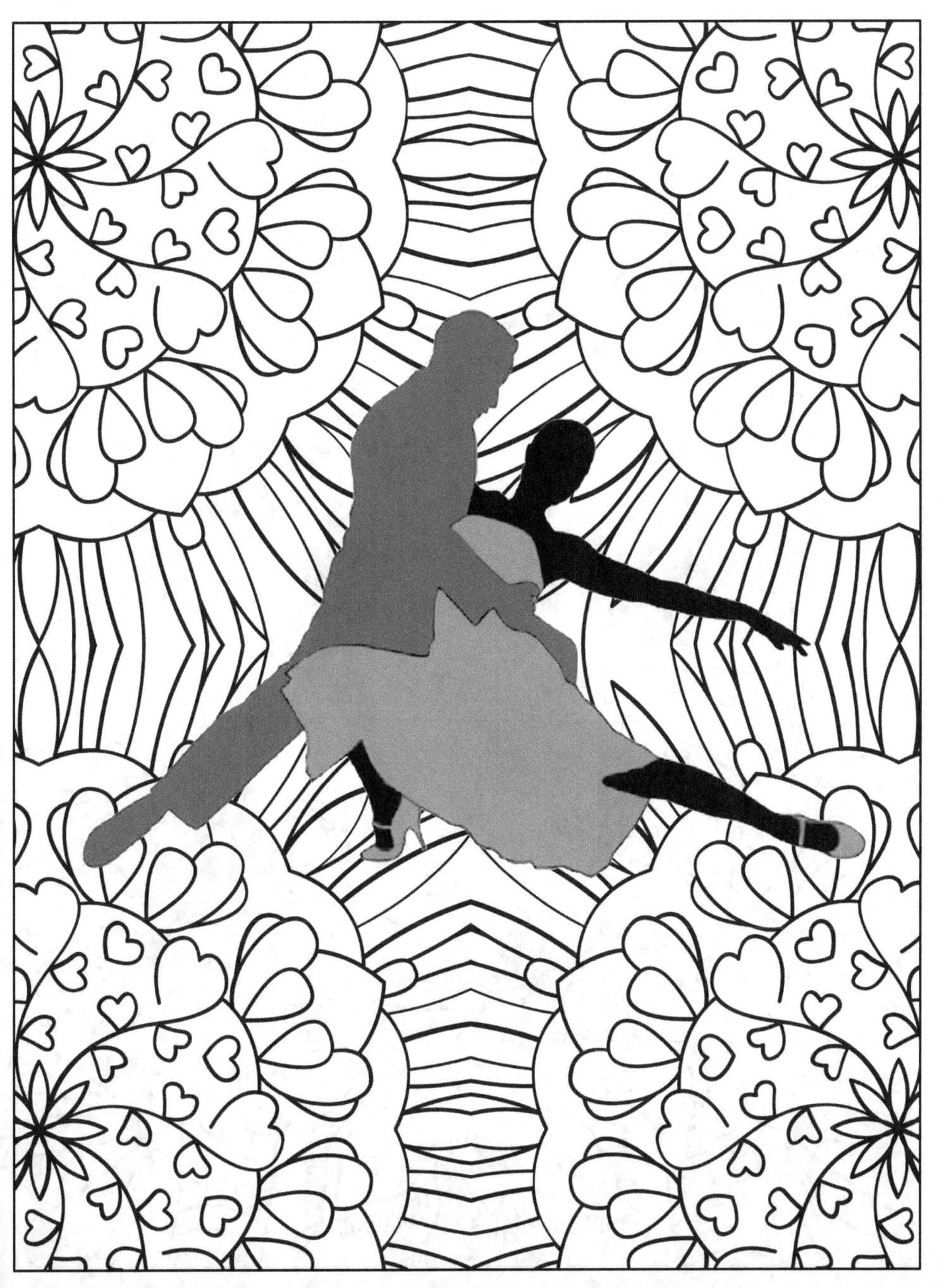

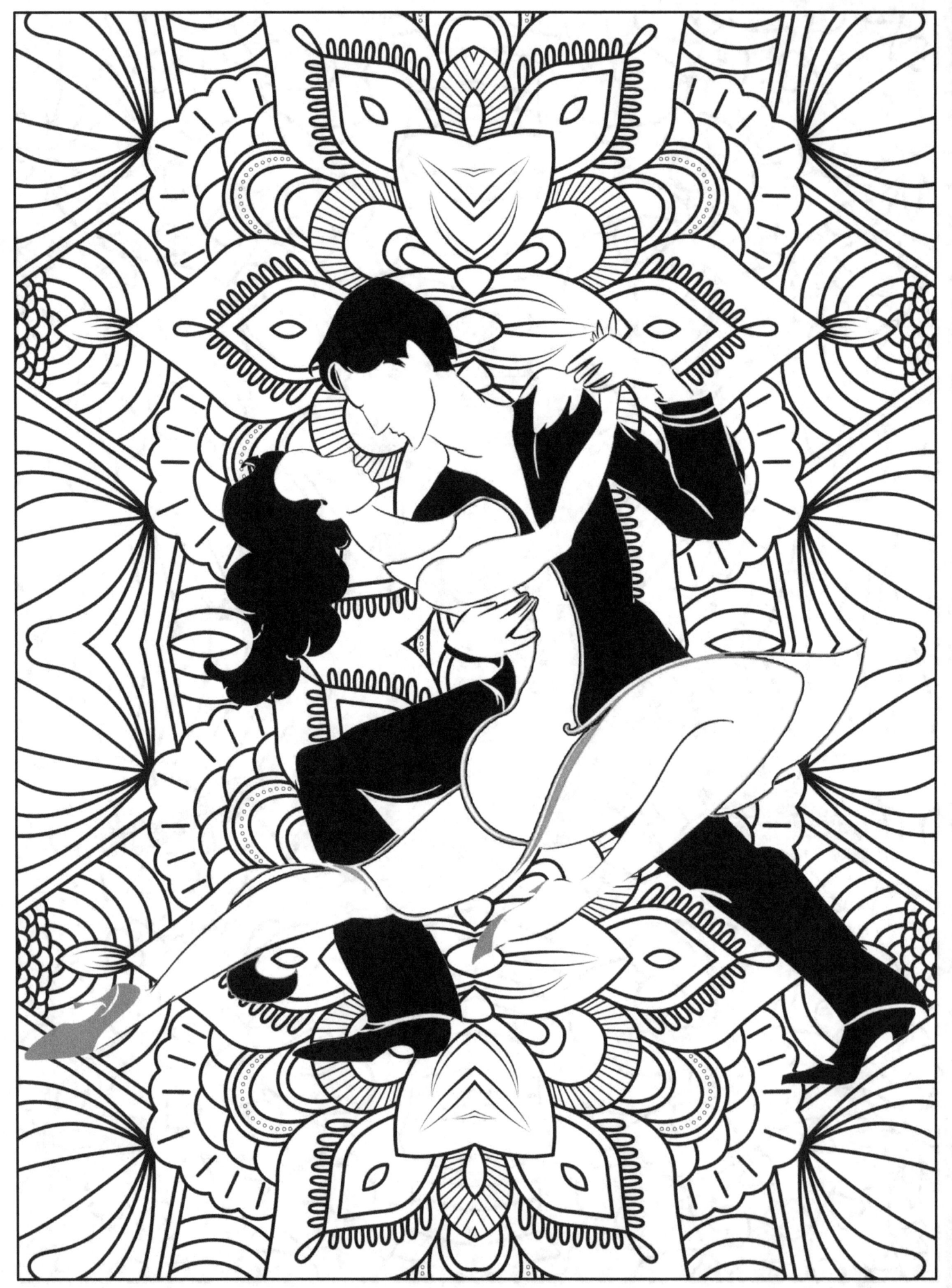

Thank you for choosing Ryan Avas@

All our books are made taking care of all the details that may please you, trying to offer fun and quality. We want our books to bring you relaxation, well-being, and a leisure time that relieves the stress of everyday life. We hope to meet your expectations.

Do not forget to leave us your opinion
if you liked it, WE APPRECIATE IT!

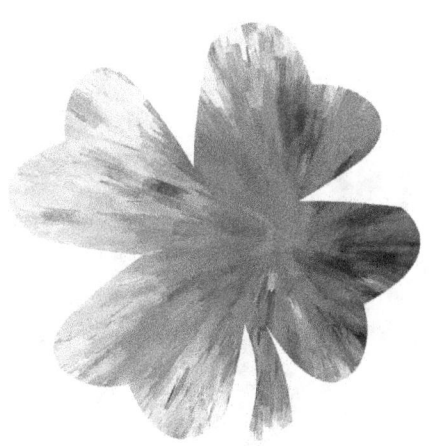